Workplace 2030

Generation Alpha Shapes the Future

By
Avery Stone

Workplace 2030

Generation Alpha Shapes the Future

Table of Contents

Embracing
a New Era

Let's face it: the workforce is on the brink of a remarkable transformation. The dawn of Generation Alpha signals not just a change in the calendar but a shift in the very fabric of our professional lives. Born roughly between 2010 and 2025, these digital natives are set to revolutionise how we work, lead, and innovate. As forward-thinking leaders, HR professionals, and strategists, the future demands we understand this emerging generation to effectively harness their potential and drive our organisations forward.

Generation Alpha is more than just the newest cohort; they represent the first generation to be completely born in the 21st century. With that comes a unique set of traits, skills, and values shaped by an era of rapid technological advancements, environmental challenges, and a globally connected society. To succeed in integrating Generation Alpha into the workplace, we must embrace their digital fluency, social consciousness, and inherent adaptability. This journey begins with accepting that change is not only inevitable but essential for growth.

Consider this: by 2030, Generation Alpha will start to enter the workforce in significant numbers. They will carry with them an unparalleled proficiency in technology, having grown up with smartphones, AI assistants, and immersive virtual environments. This digital genesis places them ahead of any prior generation in terms of tech-savviness. However, this is not just about their ability to use

1

gadgets; it's about leveraging digital tools to foster innovation and drive productivity. We must prepare to build on this foundation.

Outside of their technological prowess, Generation Alpha brings a heightened awareness of sustainability and social responsibility. They have been raised in a world where climate change and social justice movements are front-page news. This awareness translates into core values that will impact how they choose employers and engage with work. Corporations will need to demonstrate genuine commitment to environmental stewardship and social equity to attract and retain this socially conscious generation. This isn't just good ethics; it's good business.

Integrating Generation Alpha into the workforce isn't just about understanding their characteristics; it involves creating a multi-generational workplace where communication and collaboration thrive. Today's workforce spans multiple generations, from Boomers to Millennials, each with distinct traits and preferences. Our challenge lies in bridging these gaps, fostering an environment where different generations can learn from one another and work collectively towards common goals.

Imagine a workplace where inclusivity is the norm, not the exception. A key aspect of this integration involves evolving our language and communication practices to be more inclusive. This means recognising the diverse experiences and perspectives that each generation brings and finding ways to ensure that everyone's voice is heard. Inclusivity is not a checkbox; it's a continuous effort that enriches the workplace and drives innovation.

As we transition into this new era, the physical workspace itself is undergoing a transformation. Traditional offices are giving way to flexible and innovative environments that cater to the diverse needs of a modern workforce. Remote and hybrid work models are becoming the norm, spurred by the global pandemic and the evolving needs of employees. Generation Alpha will expect—and deserve—workspaces that foster creativity, collaboration, and well-being.

From an environmental perspective, sustainable practices are no longer optional. They are imperative for any business aiming to stay relevant. Green offices and eco-friendly initiatives contribute to employee well-being and productivity, making them a key consideration in designing future workspaces. Incorporating such practices will not only appeal to Generation Alpha but will set a precedent for future generations as well.

Technology and innovation are at the heart of this new era. The ongoing AI revolution presents both opportunities and challenges. Integrating AI into daily operations will require us to navigate ethical considerations and maintain job security, ensuring that automation enhances rather than displaces human roles. Embracing emerging technologies like virtual and augmented reality will also play a pivotal role in shaping the future of work, particularly in training and development.

Leadership paradigms are also shifting to address the evolving needs of the workforce. Generation Alpha will expect leaders who are adaptable, empathetic, and capable of fostering a culture of inno-vation. Moving from traditional hierarchies to network-based power dynamics will encourage risk-taking and learning from failure, essential traits in an ever-changing world. Recognising and rewarding inno-vation will be paramount for maintaining motivation and engagement among Generation Alpha employees.

Education and continuous learning will play a critical role in preparing for the future. As industries evolve, so must the skills and competencies of the workforce. There's a growing emphasis on STEM disciplines, but soft skills like communication, creativity, and critical thinking are equally crucial. Employers will need to support lifelong learning through microlearning opportunities and online platforms, ensuring that their teams stay relevant in a rapidly changing world.

With the rise of the gig economy and freelancing, traditional employment models are being redefined. Generation Alpha is likely to be drawn to the flexibility and freedom of gig work, but this presents challenges and opportunities for both workers and employers. Building a supportive framework for freelancers, including legal rights and social protections, will be essential in this new economic landscape.

Diversity, equity, and inclusion (DEI) are more than buzzwords; they are critical components of a thriving workplace. Genuine inclusion strategies that address unconscious bias and promote equity will be essential in creating an inclusive climate for Generation Alpha. DEI initiatives are not just about doing the right thing; they provide a competitive advantage by fostering innovation and bringing varied perspectives to the table.

Mental and physical health are increasingly becoming focal points in the workplace. Strategies to support mental health and resilience, alongside encouraging physical activity and work-life balance, are crucial. Leaders play a pivotal role in fostering a healthy environment, and flexible schedules can contribute significantly to maintaining this balance. Generation Alpha will expect workplaces that prioritise their overall well-being, both mentally and physically.

As we navigate the legal and ethical landscapes, data privacy and security will remain paramount. Protecting employee information, complying with regulations, and maintaining transparency and accountability in decision-making are essential aspects of a responsible business. Ethical considerations in AI and automation must be addressed to ensure that technological efficiency aligns with our moral responsibilities.

The unpredictability of the future necessitates agile methodologies and scenario planning. Adapting to change and fostering resilience are key components of preparing for uncertain times. Encouraging collaboration, experimentation, and learning from both failures and successes will help build a culture of innovation and adaptability.

Generation Alpha will bring with them a global perspective, necessitating effective management of cross-cultural teams. Building trust and accountability in remote teams, overcoming time zone challenges, and leveraging global talents are essential for competitive advantage. This new era will see unprecedented opportunities for international collaboration and growth.

As we usher in this new era, we have a unique opportunity to align our corporate values with the expectations of Generation Alpha. Environmental sustainability, social impact, and genuine community engagement will take centre stage. Measuring impact beyond profits, maintaining transparency in CSR efforts, and committing to long-term sustainable growth will resonate deeply with this new generation.

We stand on the cusp of an exciting and transformative period. Understanding and preparing for the significant changes Generation Alpha will bring to the workplace will not only secure our future but pave the way for a thriving, innovative, and sustainable world. Embrace this change, and let's get ready to forge a path into a bright new era.

Chapter 1:
Understanding Generation Alpha

As we step into the dynamic realm of Generation Alpha, it's crucial to grasp the unique characteristics and values that define these digital natives. Born from 2010 onwards, Generation Alpha is the first to grow up in a world saturated with advanced technology, fostering a level of digital fluency unparalleled by previous generations. Yet, their identities are shaped by more than just screens and devices; they possess a deep-seated commitment to sustainability and social responsibility, prioritising equitable and eco-friendly practices in ways that are set to revolutionise the workplace. Their upbringing amidst global movements and environmental consciousness has imbued them with a collective sense of purpose and a demand for meaningful work. As leaders and strategists, understanding these core aspects of Generation Alpha will not only help bridge generational gaps but enable the creation of workplaces where innovation, flexibility, and sustainability thrive, ushering in an era of unprecedented collaboration and growth.

The Birth of the Alpha: Characteristics and Values

The advent of Generation Alpha marks a pivotal shift in the landscape of future workplaces, driven by a unique set of characteristics and values that distinguish them from previous generations. Born entirely in the 21st century, members of Generation Alpha are technological natives, growing up with an innate understanding of digital devices and the internet. This comfort with technology fosters their propensity for rapid learning and adaptability, key traits that will serve them well in dynamic professional environments. Highly value-driven, Generation Alpha places a strong emphasis on sustainability and social responsibility, reflecting a broader global consciousness about the planet's future. They exhibit a profound sense of urgency and commitment towards addressing environmental issues, social justice, and ethical business practices. As we prepare to welcome Generation Alpha into our teams, it's essential to recognise that their approach isn't merely a fleeting trend but a fundamental shift that aligns closely with future-focused visions of innovation, inclusivity, and long-term sustainability.

A Digital Genesis: Technological Natives defines Generation Alpha's entry into the world, not merely as infants born into diverse families but as the very first cohort to grow up in a world where technology isn't an accessory; it's an extension of their existence. At the crux of this technological genesis lies a profound understanding that sets Generation Alpha apart from any preceding generation. What's fascinating, however, isn't just their familiarity with technology. It's their intuitive grasp and seamless integration into their daily lives that makes them bona fide digital natives.

Born from 2010 onwards, these children haven't known a world without touchscreens, voice assistants, or high-speed internet. For them, digital tools are as natural as breathing. Their interaction with technology starts almost immediately—as toddlers swiping through tablets, engaging in educational apps, and occasionally being 'naughty' with smart home devices. This constant exposure has reshaped their learning experiences, problem-solving methods, and even social interactions.

Now, what does this mean for the modern workplace? For starters, by the time Generation Alpha starts entering the workforce, traditional onboarding processes will likely be obsolete. These individuals will expect immersive virtual reality (VR) orientations, AI-driven personalised learning modules, and seamless access to remote work options right from day one. Organisations must adapt to these expectations to harness their potential effectively.

The realm of communication for Generation Alpha transcends emails and phone calls. They're proficient in leveraging real-time messaging platforms, video calls, and collaborative digital workspaces. Importantly, they value prompt and concise communication. For businesses, this means integrating platforms that support these rapid interaction styles, moving away from cumbersome hierarchical communication processes.

Having said that, one cannot underestimate the impact of social media awareness on Gen Alpha. These digital natives have grown up understanding and managing digital footprints, often better than some adults. They are conflicted by privacy, security, and transparency issues, which are no longer mere concerns but prerequisites for engaging with a brand or employer. Business leaders must ensure organisational transparency, clear data privacy practices, and robust cybersecurity measures to gain their trust.

Another crucial aspect to consider is their approach to learning and development. Generation Alpha prefers interactive, gamified learning experiences over traditional methods. Companies that incorporate AR and VR in their training programs, and adopt micro-learning strategies, will not only find it easier to engage this generation but also reap the benefits of increased knowledge retention and practical application.

But it's not just about the individual; it's about the environment they thrive in. Flexibility will be key. Although we'll delve into the specifics of remote and hybrid working models in subsequent chapters, it's essential to note here that Generation Alpha's familiarity with virtual environments means they'll demand flexibility in work locations, hours, and even roles. Traditional 9-to-5 schedules and rigid office spaces may soon find themselves relegated to history books.

Adaptive technology will become an integral part of productivity tools. With AI-driven software, Generation Alpha will expect personalised task management, intelligent assistants, and real-time analytics to guide decision-making processes. Understanding this, forward-thinking companies should start integrating such tools now to ensure seamless transitions when Gen Alpha enters the workforce.

Moreover, the collaborative nature of this generation is unparalleled. They've grown up engaging in multiplayer online games, forums, and global communities. This innate sense of collaboration, unbounded by geographical limitations, will transform teamwork dynamics. Remote collaboration tools, cloud-based project management systems, and global time management solutions must be the new norm. Businesses need to anticipate these shifts and preemptively adopt these technologies to foster highly effective, collaborative teams.

In terms of leadership, Generation Alpha will seek leaders who understand their digital world. Leaders need to be tech-savvy, adaptable, and empathetic. The hierarchical command-and-control leadership model will give way to more fluid, network-centric leadership styles that resonate with digital natives. Emotional intelligence will be paramount for leaders to connect authentically with this new cohort.

Let's not overlook the importance of social responsibility and ethical considerations about technology usage. Generation Alpha is growing up amid climate crises and social upheaval, shaping their values and priorities. There will be an expectation for corporations to not only leverage technology for profit but also for societal good. As we'll explore sustainability and social responsibility in further detail, it's crucial to begin aligning corporate strategies with these emerging values.

So, how can organisations prepare for this brave new digital world? Begin by assessing current technological infrastructures, identifying gaps, and investing in future-proof solutions. Encourage a culture of continuous learning and adaptability, ensuring that all employees, irrespective of their generational cohort, are on a perpetual learning curve. Engage in open dialogues with young digital pioneers to understand their needs and aspirations better, incorporating their feedback into long-term strategies.

In essence, the seamless integration and intuition of Generation Alpha into the digital realm create a transformative opportunity for workplaces. By understanding and embracing this digital genesis, companies can foster innovation, boost productivity, and build resilient, future-ready organisations. The time to act is now for the leaders, HR professionals, and strategists who aim to harness the full potential of Generation Alpha.

Sustainability and Social Responsibility: Core Values are not just buzzwords for Generation Alpha; they are fundamental principles that will shape their workplace behaviours and expectations. Born into a world facing critical environmental and social challenges, Gen Alpha will naturally gravitate towards organisations that prioritise these values. Companies that fail to integrate sustainability and social responsibility into their core operations may find themselves struggling to attract and retain top talent from this generation.

Generation Alpha's unwavering commitment to sustainability stems from a deep-seated awareness of environmental issues, largely influenced by their digital upbringing. These individuals have been exposed to a steady stream of information highlighting climate change, resource depletion, and ecological degradation from a very young age. As a result, they will expect their employers to take definitive actions such as reducing carbon footprints, minimising waste, and adopting renewable energy sources. Corporations will need to align their practices with these values, not as an afterthought, but as a central component of their business strategy.

Social responsibility is equally crucial to Gen Alpha. They are acutely aware of social injustices and inequality and will look for organisations that are not only aware of these issues but are actively working to address them. Corporate initiatives that promote diversity, equity, and inclusion, provide fair wages, and actively engage in comm-unity support will resonate strongly with them. Generation Alpha won't just want companies to pay lip service to these issues; they'll demand tangible evidence of commitment and impact.

An important aspect of sustainability and social responsibility is transparency. Generation Alpha places high value on honesty and openness. They have grown up with the internet at their fingertips, giving them unprecedented access to information and the means to verify claims made by organisations. Companies will need to provide clear, transparent reports on their sustainability efforts and social initiatives. Greenwashing, or making misleading claims about a company's environmental practices, simply won't cut it. Gen Alpha will scrutinise every detail, and those failing to live up to their promises will quickly lose credibility.

Furthermore, the concept of sustainability extends beyond environmental concerns to encompass economic sustainability. Gene-ration Alpha will be discerning about the financial health and ethical stance of their employers. Organisations that balance economic performance with environmental stewardship and social responsibility will be seen as forward-thinking and trustworthy. This holistic view of sustainability will drive companies to adopt long-term strategies that consider the well-being of various stakeholders, not just shareholders.

Given their strong digital literacy, Generation Alpha will also push for technological innovations to support sustainability and social responsibility efforts. They'll expect companies to implement advanced technologies that enhance energy efficiency, reduce waste, and improve supply chain transparency. For instance, blockchain technology can be leveraged to ensure ethical sourcing of materials, while AI and machine learning can optimise resource use and reduce emissions.

In this evolving landscape, leaders must understand that fostering a culture of sustainability and social responsibility isn't just a top-down mandate; it involves collaborative efforts across all levels of the organisation. Empowering employees to participate in sustainability initiatives can yield significant benefits. Companies should encourage team members to propose innovative solutions, participate in green initiatives, and champion social causes. This bottom-up approach not only drives engagement but also uncovers a wealth of untapped potential within the workforce.

Moreover, sustainability and social responsibility are interlinked with corporate culture and employee well-being. Work environments that prioritise these values often see higher levels of job satisfaction and employee retention. When people feel they're contributing to something greater than themselves, it increases their sense of purpose and alignment with the organisation's mission. Thus, integrating these core values can significantly enhance overall workplace morale and productivity.

It's also worth noting that sustainability and social responsibility can open new avenues for business innovation and market opportunities. Companies that lead in these areas can differentiate themselves from competitors and appeal to a broader audience. For instance, developing eco-friendly products or services can attract environmentally conscious customers, while equitable business practices can strengthen brand loyalty and reputation.

Gaining these strategic advantages will require a shift in mindsets and practices. Companies must view sustainability and social responsibility as integral to their business models rather than peripheral concerns. This transition involves rethinking traditional metrics of success to include social and environmental impact, alongside financial performance. Forward-thinking leaders will need to pioneer this shift, setting ambitious goals and engaging stakeholders at every level.

As companies undertake these initiatives, collaboration with external partners and stakeholders becomes increasingly important. Working with non-profits, governments, and other businesses can amplify the impact of sustainability and social responsibility efforts. Generation Alpha will appreciate and support organisations that are proactive in building alliances for the greater good.

In summary, the future workplace that effectively integrates Generation Alpha will be one where sustainability and social responsibility are deeply woven into the fabric of the organisation. Companies can't afford to treat these values as mere obligations or marketing tactics. They must be seen as essential components of a resilient and thriving business. By embracing these principles, organisations not only attract Generation Alpha but also position themselves as leaders in the global drive towards a sustainable and equitable future.

As we move forward, let us remember that the pursuit of sustainability and social responsibility is a journey, not a destination. It requires continuous learning, adaptation, and a genuine commitment to making a positive impact. By fostering a workplace culture that embodies these core values, we can inspire the next generation to dream bigger, innovate smarter, and create a world that we're all proud to be a part of.

Bridging the Generation Gap: Communication and Collaboration

Creating a harmonious multi-generational workplace means fostering seamless communication and collaboration between Generation Alpha and their predecessors. This future-focused cohort, with their intuitive grasp of digital tools and profound social consciousness, will necessitate a shift in how we communicate and work together. Successfully bridging the generational gap will require leveraging their strengths while promoting mutual understanding and respect. By embracing flexible, inclusive communication practices and creating collaborative opportunities such as cross-generational mentoring programmes, forward-thinking leaders can ensure that wisdom flows in both directions, fostering a workplace where innovation and shared goals flourish. More than mere coexistence, this synergy can lead to unprecedented leaps in creativity and effectiveness, positioning organisations to not only adapt to but thrive amidst the rapid changes of tomorrow.

From Boomers to Alphas: A Multi-Generational Workplace presents an intriguing challenge and opportunity for today's forward-thinking leaders. In workplaces where Baby Boomers, Generation X, Millennials, and Generation Z have been collaborating for years, Generation Alpha's entry will mark a significant shift. To harness the potential of a multi-generational workplace, it's crucial to understand the distinct characteristics and preferences of each generation while fostering an environment of mutual respect and collaboration.

Baby Boomers, born between 1946 and 1964, are often characterised by their strong work ethic and loyalty to their employers. They favour face-to-face communication and value hierarchical structures. Conversely, Generation X, born between 1965 and 1980, are known for their independence and pragmatic approach. Their adaptability to technological changes has made them pivotal in driving digital transformations within organisations.

Millennials, or Generation Y, who were born between 1981 and 1996, brought a demand for work-life balance and have been the driving force behind flexible working arrangements. Their preference for collaborative work environments and emphasis on purpose-driven careers have reshaped corporate cultures across the globe. Generation Z, the cohort born between 1997 and 2012, entered the workforce with an innate understanding of digital technologies and a strong inclination towards inclusivity and social responsibility.

Enter Generation Alpha, a group destined to redefine workplaces once more. Born from 2013 onward, these digital natives will bring unparalleled technological fluency and an expectation for a sustainable, inclusive workplace. They are growing up in an era where artificial intelligence, virtual reality, and robotics are part of the household lexicon. As educators and futurists predict, Generation Alpha will prioritise innovation, flexibility, and meaningful work experiences.

In a multi-generational workplace, the key to success lies in leveraging the strengths of each generation. The first step is understanding the unique communication styles and preferences each generation brings. While Boomers may prefer formal, in-person discussions, Alphas will likely feel more at home with digital communication tools such as augmented reality meetings or AI-driven collaboration platforms.

Inclusivity in communication isn't just about the medium; it's about the message. Leaders must employ strategies that respect and incorporate the viewpoints of every generation. Creating open channels for feedback and encouraging cross-generational mentorship can bridge gaps and enhance collective intelligence. By blending traditional modes of operation with cutting-edge technology, organisations can foster a culture of continuous learning and adaptation.

When it comes to collaboration, it's vital to design workspaces that accommodate diverse work styles. Boomers might thrive in a structured office environment, while Alphas and Millennials may excel in flexible, remote setups. Here's where the rise of hybrid work models can play a significant role. Hybrid models allow the best of both worlds—structured in-office days and flexible remote tasks—ensuring that each generation can work in their most productive settings.

Moreover, understanding the motivations driving each generation is central to fostering a harmonious workplace. Boomers and Generation X often seek stability and financial security, whereas Millennials and Gen Z value purpose and impact alongside their careers. With Generation Alpha, there will be a greater inclination towards environmental and social responsibility. They'll look up to companies not just for their success, but for their contribution to global causes.

Recognising intergenerational differences also involves appreciating the varied learning preferences. Boomers might engage more with training sessions and workshops, whereas Alphas will likely favour interactive, gamified learning platforms and microlearning modules. Embracing a multi-faceted approach to professional development can not only cater to these differences but also stimulate innovation.

Leaders must also be adaptable and empathetic. Emotional intelligence will be a cornerstone trait for leaders navigating the complexities of a multi-generational workforce. Demonstrating appreciation for the experiences and knowledge of older generations while championing the fresh perspectives of younger workers can create a balanced and forward-thinking workplace.

Encouraging intergenerational teams is another practical strategy. When Boomers' decades of experience are combined with Alphas' technological savvy, you get a powerful synergy that drives productivity and innovation. Projects that promote cross-generational collaboration, accompanied by recognition and reward systems that acknowledge collective achievements, can bolster team morale and integrate diverse viewpoints.

However, there are challenges. Stereotypes and biases, whether conscious or unconscious, can undermine efforts to foster a truly inclusive workplace. Training to address and counteract these biases is essential. When employees see that their contributions are valued irrespective of age, it fosters a sense of belonging and trust.

For HR professionals, anticipating the needs and expectations of Generation Alpha will be crucial. Implementing flexible policies, offering continuous learning opportunities, and promoting a healthy work-life balance are steps in the right direction. It's also vital to use technology not just as a tool for productivity but as a bridge connecting generations.

The ultimate goal for organisations is to create a workspace where all generations feel valued and empowered. This requires an ongoing dialogue, a genuine appreciation for diversity, and a commitment to cultivating an environment where innovation thrives. In doing so, companies can leverage the collective strengths of a multigenerational workforce to not just meet, but exceed, the challenges of the future.

In conclusion, integrating Generation Alpha into a multigenerational workplace isn't just about preparing for the future; it's about enriching the present. By fostering an inclusive, adaptable, and innovative culture, organisations can ensure that they're not only ready for what's to come but are also capable of leading the charge into a new era of work.

Language and Communication: Evolving for Inclusivity is at the heart of integrating Generation Alpha into the workplace. This generation, born from 2010 onwards, has grown up immersed in technology, sensitivity to global issues, and an ethos that celebrates diversity. The way we communicate with and among these digital natives will evolve significantly. To truly embrace inclusivity, our language and communication practices must reflect the values of empathy, equality, and openness that define Generation Alpha.

Generation Alpha communicates in a world where emojis, GIFs, and instant messaging are not just commonplace but essential. These forms of communication transcend language barriers and offer a new dimension to express emotions and ideas succinctly. In the workplace, traditional email may give way to more dynamic forms of interaction. Instant messaging platforms, video calls, and collaborative work environments that allow real-time feedback and interaction can foster inclusiveness and collaboration.

Inclusivity goes beyond just adopting new communication tools. It involves ensuring that language itself is inclusive. Language that recognises and respects all gender identities, cultural backgrounds and abilities is non-negotiable. Using gender-neutral terms, avoiding assumptions based on race or nationality, and being mindful of unconscious biases in everyday speech contribute to creating a more inclusive and welcoming workspace for Generation Alpha.

The vernacular of the workplace is also shifting. For a start, keywords and phrases once centred on competition and hierarchy are being replaced with those that emphasise collaboration and flat structures. Terms like "team effort" and "collective success" resonate more with Generation Alpha, who value cooperation and mutual respect over cutthroat competitiveness. Leaders must embody this shift in discourse to truly connect with and motivate their teams.

Open communication is crucial. Generation Alpha expects to be heard and values transparency from their leaders and peers. Regular updates, open forums, and active solicitation of feedback can make Alphas feel included and valued. Information should flow both ways in a candid and supportive manner. This generation isn't inclined to accept hierarchical communication where bosses speak and employees listen quietly. They crave a dialogue where their voice influences the collective direction.

Furthermore, communication is not just about talking but listening. Active listening—where leaders and colleagues genuinely pay attention, show empathy, and take action based on the feedback received—is foundational. When communication practices underscore respect and active listening, workplaces become breeding grounds for innovation and inclusivity.

Another change in the communication landscape is the emphasis on visual and auditory elements. Video messages, interactive dashboards, and graphical presentations become potent tools to convey information effectively and engagingly. Generation Alpha, with their affinity for visual content, can grasp complex ideas more swiftly with well-designed graphics and videos. Incorporating these forms into regular communication can break down barriers and enhance understanding.

Understanding different communication styles is also vital. Generation Alpha is used to personalised experiences in almost every aspect of their lives, from social media algorithms to streaming services. This expectation carries into the workplace. Personalising communication—tailoring messages to the personal and professional contexts of each individual—can significantly enhance engagement and inclusivity. Leaders must be adept at identifying and acknowledging the diverse needs and preferences in their teams.

Diversity in communication styles also means an increased appreciation for multilingualism. As workplaces become more global, the ability to communicate across languages becomes a valuable asset. Encouraging multilingual communication, offering language learning opportunities, and respecting linguistic diversity can foster a more inclusive environment. A multilingual approach not only bridges gaps but also signals an organisation's commitment to inclusivity on a global scale.

Another critical consideration is accessibility. An inclusive language policy must cater to employees with disabilities. Written communication should be accessible to those using screen readers, and visual content should include descriptive text. Meetings should consider the needs of those who use sign language or need real-time captions. Inclusivity in communication means that everyone, regardless of their physical abilities, can participate fully and meaningfully.

The influence of social media cannot be overstated. Generation Alpha has been raised in an era where social media platforms are significant communication channels. Organisations that leverage social media for internal communication can tap into the familiarity and comfort that Gen Alpha has with these platforms. Social media can also serve as a tool for recognising achievements, sharing updates, and building a sense of community.

Narrative-building and storytelling will play central roles in future workplace communication. Generation Alpha values authenticity and relatable storytelling over polished corporate jargon. Leaders who can weave compelling narratives that align with the personal values and professional aspirations of their teams will build stronger, more inclusive relationships. Stories that highlight diverse voices and experiences will resonate deeply and foster a culture of inclusivity.

It's also essential to consider the role of empathy in communication. Empathic communication recognises the feelings and experiences of others and responds in supportive and constructive ways. This involves not only what is said but how it is said. Tone, body language, and choice of words all convey empathy and respect. Training in empathic communication can equip leaders and employees with the skills needed to create a more inclusive workplace.

Lastly, evolving communication for inclusivity requires ongoing commitment and education. It's not a one-time effort but a continuous process of self-reflection, learning, and adaptation. Organisations should invest in regular training and workshops that focus on inclusive language and communication. This will ensure that the principles of inclusivity are ingrained in the workplace culture and practice.

In sum, evolving language and communication for inclusivity is a multifaceted endeavour that demands attention to new communication tools, inclusive language practices, active listening, personalisation, accessibility, multilingualism, and empathy. By embracing these changes, leaders and HR professionals can build a workplace where Generation Alpha thrives, contributing to a future defined by collaboration, innovation, and inclusivity.

Chapter 2:
The Transformation of Workspaces

As Generation Alpha steps into the professional world, the essence of workspaces is poised for a remarkable transformation. Traditional offices, with their rigid layouts and standardised setups, are giving way to dynamic environments that prioritise flexibility, innovation, and well-being. Remote and hybrid models are no longer exceptions but rather integral parts of the contemporary workspace, fostering a culture where creativity and productivity flourish regardless of physical location. Innovative office designs are introducing collaborative spaces that inspire teamwork and inventive thinking, while the focus on sustainability is prompting a shift towards green offices that not only minimise environmental impact but also enhance employee health and job satisfaction. This evolution is about more than just changing physical spaces—it's about redefining the very concept of work to align with the values of a new generation that demands adaptability, eco-consciousness, and a holistic approach to productivity. For forward-thinking leaders, HR professionals, and strategists, recognising and adapting to these changes isn't merely beneficial—it's essential to cultivating a workplace where Generation Alpha can thrive and drive future successes.

Beyond The Traditional Office: Flexibility and Innovation

The days of rigid nine-to-five office schedules and static cubicles are evolving into something far more dynamic and inspiring. Generation Alpha's entry into the workforce necessitates an environment where innovation and flexibility not only coexist but thrive. This means rethinking the traditional office to embrace remote and hybrid work models, creating spaces that nurture creativity and foster collaboration. Forward-thinking leaders and HR professionals must consider how to design workspaces that are not just places of productivity, but also hubs of innovation and inclusivity. Imagine flexible schedules that cater to individual needs and multi-functional areas that can effortlessly switch from brainstorming sessions to quiet zones for focussed work. These changes are not just about keeping up with trends, but about building workplaces that attract and retain the best talent while encouraging a culture of continuous learning and creativity. It's not just the work we do that's changing; it's also how and where we do it, paving the way for a future that's as adaptable as it is exciting.

The Rise of Remote and Hybrid Models encapsulates a profound shift in the way we work. It's more than just a fleeting trend; it represents a fundamental transformation in workspace design and management. The Generation Alpha workforce, characterized by their seamless integration with digital technologies, is driving this shift as they enter the workplace. Traditional notions of office spaces are being redefined, marking the onset of an era where flexibility and adaptability are paramount.

To understand the rise of remote and hybrid models, we need to examine the catalysts that have propelled this change. Technology advancements have considerably lowered communication barriers, making it feasible for teams to collaborate across different locations as effectively as they would in the same office. Video conferencing, project management tools, and cloud computing are now staples in modern workplaces, enabling a fluid work environment that Generation Alpha both expects and excels in.

This shift has been influenced significantly by the global pandemic, which forced organisations worldwide to adopt remote work as a necessity rather than an option. This critical period demonstrated that productivity isn't tied to a physical location; indeed, in many cases, productivity levels remained steady or even improved. Companies realised the potential of remote work, not just as a contingency plan, but as a viable long-term strategy.

Remote and hybrid models offer several critical benefits such as increased employee satisfaction. Many employees appreciate the autonomy and flexibility that comes with remote work. It allows for a better work-life balance, reducing commuter fatigue and giving workers the ability to structure their day in a way that suits their personal and professional needs.

However, it's not just about working from home. The hybrid model, which combines both remote and in-office work, seems to strike an optimal balance. It affords employees the flexibility they crave while maintaining the social and collaborative benefits of being in a shared workspace. This flexibility is likely to be a substantial draw for Generation Alpha, who value individuality and customisation in their professional lives.

That being said, transitioning to these models requires mindful planning. Organisations must overcome challenges related to accountability, team cohesion, and maintaining corporate culture. Effective leadership is vital in this transition, ensuring that remote and hybrid teams remain engaged and connected. Leaders must give extra attention to clear communication, trust-building, and developing a strong sense of community among geographically dispersed teams.

One approach is to leverage technology that not only supports remote work but also fosters collaboration and innovation. Digital tools such as Slack, Trello, and Microsoft Teams can play a pivotal role in this context. Employing advanced collaboration platforms helps maintain workflows and encourages spontaneous, creative interactions even when team members are scattered across different locations.

Employee well-being is another critical aspect. While remote work provides flexibility, it can also lead to isolation and burnout if not managed properly. Organisations must therefore develop robust support systems, offering resources for mental health, professional development, and virtual social activities. Creating regular check-ins and fostering open lines of communication can also mitigate some of these challenges.

There's also a need to rethink performance evaluations in a remote or hybrid context. Traditional metrics that rely on physical presence and 'face time' won't be valid indicators of productivity and contribution. Instead, focusing on outcomes and deliverables will provide a more accurate picture of employee performance and help align expectations appropriately.

These new models bring implications for office spaces themselves. As remote and hybrid models become more entrenched, companies are re-evaluating the need and design for physical offices. Many are opting for coworking spaces or downsizing their offices, creating vibrant, multi-purpose hubs designed for collaboration, innovation, and social interaction rather than day-to-day tasks better suited for remote work.

Furthermore, this shift supports sustainability goals. Reduced commuting means lower carbon emissions, aligning with the values of Generation Alpha, who prioritise sustainability. Hybrid work models thus present a win-win scenario, supporting environmental goals while meeting employee desires for flexibility and autonomy.

The rise of remote and hybrid models also brings a global dimension to the workforce. Geographical boundaries are less of a constraint, enabling organisations to tap into talent pools across the world. This global perspective can be a strategic advantage, bringing diverse viewpoints and fostering a more inclusive and innovative workplace.

In conclusion, the rise of remote and hybrid models represents more than just a change in where people work; it's a paradigm shift in how organisations operate and engage with their employees. Generation Alpha, with their unique characteristics and values, are at the forefront of this transformation. Organisations that embrace these changes and adequately prepare for the nuances associated with remote and hybrid work will be well-positioned to attract and retain the emerging talent pool, fostering a future where innovation, flexibility, and sustainability thrive.

Designing Spaces for Creativity and Collaboration is crucial as we move into an era where Generation Alpha starts making their mark in the workplace. Unlike previous generations, Generation Alpha has grown up in a world saturated with technology, social cone-ctivity, and unprecedented access to information. These factors have shaped their expectations and behaviours, especially in the workplace. To fully harness their potential, businesses must seriously consider how to design spaces that foster creativity and facilitate seamless collaboration.

First, let's consider the physical layout. Historically, the archetype of an office has evolved from private cubicles to open-plan spaces. Although open offices have sometimes faced criticism for being too noisy or distracting, they offer a significant advantage in fostering collaboration. Generation Alpha thrives in an environment where they can easily communicate and exchange ideas; hence, a well-balanced mix of open spaces and quiet zones can offer the best of both worlds.

Next, we delve into the importance of flexibility within these spaces. Flexibility isn't merely about having adjustable seating but incorporates adaptable environments that can easily be reconfigured for different tasks. Movable walls, modular furniture, and multi-purpose areas can all contribute to a dynamic workspace. By doing this, companies empower employees to adopt the space to fit their needs, whether that's a brainstorming session, quiet work, or a team meeting.

Technological integration is another key factor. Interactive whiteboards, video conferencing tools, and collaborative software platforms should be embedded within the workspace. Given Generation Alpha's seamless interaction with technology, these tools will be second nature to them. They can easily switch from a physical collaboration in the office to virtual teamwork if necessary, thereby transcending geographical limitations.

Creating spaces that inspire is equally important. The ambiance and aesthetics of a work environment can greatly impact creativity and productivity. Vibrant colours, natural lighting, and inspiring decor contribute to a stimulating work atmosphere. Artistic elements and spaces designed with biophilia in mind—integrating natural elements into the design—can make the office not only a place of work but also an environment where creativity can flourish.

Let's not underestimate the power of social spaces. Areas designed for informal gatherings, such as lounges or coffee corners, can encourage spontaneous interactions, which are often the breeding grounds for creative ideation. A casual conversation over coffee can quickly turn into the next big project or initiative. This spontaneity can be a game-changer, aligning perfectly with Generation Alpha's intrinsic connectivity and social interaction.

Spaces that promote well-being and mental health are also critical. Introducing areas for relaxation, such as meditation rooms or wellness zones, provides employees with the opportunity to recharge. For Generation Alpha, who value a balanced lifestyle and mental health, these spaces signal that their employer cares about their holistic well-being, which can, in turn, enhance loyalty and productivity.

Beyond the physical environment, a culture that encourages creativity and collaboration is indispensable. Leadership plays a significant role in this. Leaders must cultivate an atmosphere of trust and openness, where employees feel comfortable sharing ideas without fear of judgement. An open-door policy, regular brainstorming sessions, and workshops focused on innovative thinking can all contribute to this culture.

Training and development tailored to Generation Alpha's strengths and preferences will also help. This generation is accustomed to interactive and engaging learning experiences. Incorporating virtual reality for training sessions, gamified learning modules, and peer-to-peer learning opportunities can keep them engaged and motivated.

Moreover, think about mentorship opportunities. Mixed-age teams can offer diverse perspectives, fostering richer, more holistic creative outputs. Generation Alpha can benefit from the experience and wisdom of older employees while bringing their own fresh, tech-savvy insights to the table. In turn, such practices help in bridging the generation gap while promoting mutual respect and understanding.

The environmental impact of workspaces cannot be ignored, especially given Generation Alpha's strong inclination towards sustainability. Energy-efficient buildings, waste reduction programs, and eco-friendly designs are not just add-ons but essential components of a modern, forward-thinking workspace. Such practices not only reduce operational costs but also align with the values of younger employees, making them feel part of a responsible and progressive organisation.

An interesting concept to experiment with is 'activity-based working' where employees are not tied to a specific desk but can choose their workspace based on the task at hand. This involves creating various zones within the office—a quiet zone, a collaborative zone, a learning zone, and even a play zone. Such an arrangement caters to the diverse tasks employees might need to undertake during the day, thereby enhancing flexibility and productivity.

As enterprises move towards hybrid and remote working models, the importance of the physical office space becomes even more pronounced. These spaces must offer compelling reasons for employees to come into the office. Designing hubs for creativity and collaboration ensures that when employees do come in, they find value in the physical workspace that they cannot find in a remote setup.

Incorporating feedback from Generation Alpha into the design process is another useful strategy. Who better to inform the creation of these spaces than the people who will use them? Regularly gathering and acting on employee input sends a clear message that the company values their opinions and is committed to providing an optimal work environment.

Ultimately, the goal is to create an environment that doesn't just accommodate Generation Alpha but actively enhances their strengths and engages their uniquely digital and collaborative natures. The workspace should be a reflection of the values of innovation, flexibility, and sustainability. Aligning physical design with organisational culture is crucial to fostering a thriving workplace for Generation Alpha and beyond.

Environmental Considerations: A Sustainable Workspace

As we rethink the modern workspace, sustainability can't just be an afterthought; it's got to be a core principle. Forward-thinking organisations understand that an eco-friendly office isn't just good for the planet—it's great for employee morale and productivity too. By integrating green practices such as energy-efficient lighting, sustainable materials, and waste reduction programs, we can create work environments that reflect Generation Alpha's strong values around environmental stewardship. Sustainable workspaces inspire innovation, reduce overhead costs, and signal to the workforce and clients alike that your organisation is committed to more than just profit—it's dedicated to making a meaningful impact. When we build spaces that care for the earth, we cultivate a culture of responsibility and forward-thinking that will be the hallmark of successful enterprises in the years to come.

Green Offices and Eco-Friendly Practices are not just trendy buzzwords; they're essential strategies for the workplace of tomorrow. As we prepare to integrate Generation Alpha into our environments, it's crucial to understand their intrinsic values, particularly when it comes to sustainability. This chapter will explore how embracing green offices and eco-friendly practices can align with the aspirations of Generation Alpha, foster a productive work atmosphere, and present a beacon of corporate responsibility.

Generation Alpha is stepping into a world where environmental consciousness isn't optional but mandatory. Thus, companies that wish to attract and retain these emerging talents must prioritise green initiatives. This approach isn't limited to reducing carbon footprints; it extends to creating workspaces that are designed for sustainability at their core. From energy-efficient lighting to waste reduction strategies, every element plays a role.

Consider the layout and construction materials of the office itself. Opt for sustainable building materials such as reclaimed wood, recycled steel, and low-emission paints. These choices reflect a commitment to eco-friendly practices right from the outset and resonate deeply with Generation Alpha's ethos. Their appreciation for such measures will contribute to their workplace satisfaction and loyalty.

Moreover, adopting renewable energy sources like solar or wind power can drastically reduce a company's environmental impact. These alternatives not only cut down on greenhouse gas emissions but also offer long-term cost savings. Installing solar panels or switching to green energy providers shows a forward-thinking approach that will attract Generation Alpha's favour.

Beyond structural components, everyday office operations can contribute significantly to a sustainable environment. Implementing comprehensive recycling programs and encouraging the reduction of single-use plastics set a standard that Generation Alpha will expect. Set up recycling stations for paper, plastics, and electronic waste, and ensure these are easily accessible to all employees.

Introducing indoor plants into the office space serves dual purposes: enhancing air quality and boosting employee well-being. Plants absorb toxins and release oxygen, creating a healthier workspace. Additionally, they can increase productivity and reduce stress, aligning perfectly with Generation Alpha's preference for well-rounded well-being practices.

Office furniture and equipment should also be selected with sustainability in mind. Choose items made from recycled or recyclable materials and opt for energy-efficient electronics. Each decision, no matter how small, contributes to a larger green initiative that will not go unnoticed by Generation Alpha employees.

An essential aspect of green offices that significantly affects employee well-being is air quality. Investing in air purification systems and ensuring proper ventilation can vastly improve the indoor environment. Generation Alpha, like any modern workforce, values health and comfort, and good air quality is crucial for both.

Building a green office is not solely about the physical elements but also about fostering an eco-friendly culture. Organise workshops and training sessions to educate employees on sustainable practices both in and out of the office. Encourage initiatives such as carpooling, biking to work, or using public transport. These efforts help in building a community of environmentally conscious individuals who are collectively working towards a common goal.

Technology can play a pivotal role in promoting eco-friendly practices. Use digital tools to reduce paper usage—adopt cloud-based storage solutions, digital signatures, and online collaboration platforms. Transitioning to a paperless office not only conserves resources but also streamlines operations, making work more efficient.

Lastly, involve employees in sustainability initiatives. Form green committees to brainstorm and implement eco-friendly policies tailored to your workplace. Encourage feedback and ideas from all staff members, making them active participants in the company's sustainability journey. This sense of ownership will invigorate Generation Alpha, as they are inherently inclined towards collaborative and inclusive practices.

Green offices and eco-friendly practices offer a myriad of benefits beyond environmental impact. They enhance employee health, boost morale, and even improve work-life balance by creating more pleasant and efficient working conditions. For Generation Alpha, these practices are not mere advantages but expected norms.

Embracing green initiatives in the workplace will not only attract Generation Alpha but also set a precedent for future generations to follow. As these young professionals enter the workforce, their expectations will shape corporate landscapes, pushing companies towards more sustainable and socially responsible operations.

By fostering a green office environment, businesses can demonstrate that they are not only ready to welcome Generation Alpha but also committed to their values and well-being. The integration of eco-friendly practices is an essential step in creating a forward-thinking, sustainable, and vibrant workplace that can thrive in harmony with the planet.

Incorporating these elements into your workplace culture goes beyond just meeting the expectations of Generation Alpha; it positions your organisation as a leader in sustainability. This leadership will attract not only top talent but also clients and partners who value and seek out environmentally responsible businesses.

As we continue to adapt to the evolving needs and values of the workforce, green offices and eco-friendly practices will undoubtedly remain at the forefront. Let's not merely follow this trend but lead it with innovation, commitment, and passion for a better, sustainable future.

The Impact on Employee Well-being and Productivity in the context of Generation Alpha coming into the workplace is profound and multifaceted. As we rethink traditional office environments, the need to focus on the well-being of employees has never been more critical. Generation Alpha, with their unique characteristics and values, will reshape how we approach productivity, work-life balance, and overall job satisfaction.

One of the most significant shifts we can anticipate is the demand for flexibility. Generation Alpha, having grown up with technology that allows them to connect anytime and anywhere, will naturally expect the same from their workplaces. Flexible schedules and hybrid work models will become standard, enabling employees to manage their work in a way that complements their personal lives. This flexibility can dramatically improve well-being, reducing stress and burnout by allowing employees to work when and where they are most productive.

With flexibility comes the need for organisations to trust their employees more deeply. Trust not only strengthens organisational culture but also empowers employees to take ownership of their work. This sense of ownership can boost morale and improve productivity, as employees feel valued and recognized for their contributions. Trust and empowerment are especially critical for Generation Alpha, who value autonomy and the ability to impact their work environment meaningfully.

At the same time, the physical workspace itself will undergo transformation. Gone are the days when cubicles and closed offices dominated the landscape. Today, we see a trend towards open, collaborative spaces that encourage interaction, creativity, and innovation. For Generation Alpha, who are accustomed to highly interactive and engaging digital environments, such spaces will feel intuitive and motivating. They will thrive in settings that offer both communal areas for collaboration and quiet zones for focused work.

The emphasis on creativity and collaboration does not mean that personal space should be compromised. Generation Alpha will also demand environments that support their individual well-being. Quiet rooms, relaxation zones, and wellness centres can offer a sanctuary where employees can recharge. Integrating nature through biophilic design—such as indoor plants, natural light, and outdoor spaces—can also enhance mental health and productivity.

Technological integration is another critical facet of this transformation. Generation Alpha will expect seamless technology that supports their work without causing frustration or stress. Advanced tools for project management, communication, and virtual collaboration can make remote work more efficient and less stressful. In addition, AI and machine learning algorithms can automate mundane tasks, freeing up time for employees to focus on more meaningful and creative work.

While technology offers numerous benefits, it's essential to strike a balance to prevent potential downsides like over-reliance on digital tools or the erosion of face-to-face interactions. Establishing guidelines and frameworks that promote healthy tech use will be vital. This ensures that technology enhances rather than detracts from employee well-being.

Additionally, sustainable practices in the workplace have a substantial impact on employee well-being. Generation Alpha is deeply concerned about environmental issues, and working in an eco-friendly environment can align with their values, increasing job satisfaction. Green offices—with energy-efficient systems, recycling programs, and sustainable materials—can make employees feel part of something bigger, contributing positively to the planet.

Sustainability efforts should go beyond the physical workspace. Companies need to incorporate sustainability into their culture and operations. This could mean supporting remote work to reduce carbon footprints, encouraging the use of public transport or carpooling, and providing resources for employee wellness initiatives. When employees see their company's commitment to sustainability, it creates a sense of pride and loyalty, fostering a positive work environment.

Equally important is the focus on mental health. Generation Alpha, more than previous generations, is open about discussing mental health challenges and seeking support. Employers must prioritize mental health by offering resources such as counselling services, mental health days, and stress management workshops.

Promoting a culture where mental health is openly discussed and supported can lead to a more engaged and productive workforce.

Physical health cannot be overlooked. Encouraging physical activity, whether through on-site gyms, yoga classes, or incentives for active commuting, can improve employee health and reduce absenteeism. Ergonomically designed workstations can also reduce physical strain and improve comfort, leading to higher productivity and satisfaction.

The move towards a more holistic approach to employee well-being aligns perfectly with the values of Generation Alpha. It recognises that employees are not just workers but whole individuals with diverse needs and aspirations. By addressing these needs comprehensively, organisations can create a more motivated, loyal, and productive workforce.

Let's not forget the importance of a supportive leadership culture. Leaders who demonstrate empathy, provide regular feedback, and recognize employee achievements can foster a positive work environment. Positive reinforcement and recognition systems can motivate Generation Alpha to excel and stay engaged. Leadership must also be accessible and transparent, making young employees feel heard and valued.

Investing in continuous learning opportunities can also enhance employee well-being. Generation Alpha will look for employers who support their growth through training programs, mentoring, and resources for skill development. Lifelong learning initiatives can keep the workforce adaptive and agile, meeting the ever-evolving demands of the workplace.

In conclusion, the impact of Generation Alpha on employee well-being and productivity cannot be overstated. By embracing flexible work models, creating inspiring workspaces, integrating technology thoughtfully, and prioritising mental and physical health, organisations can not only meet the expectations of this new generation but also foster a thriving, productive workforce. The future workplace promises to be more dynamic, inclusive, and supportive, setting the stage for unprecedented innovation and growth.

Chapter 3:
Technology and Innovation

The workplace of tomorrow will be defined by the rapid assimilation of cutting-edge technologies that redefine how we perform tasks, communicate, and innovate. As Generation Alpha steps into the professional arena, their intrinsic familiarity with artificial intelligence, virtual reality, and blockchain technologies will act as a catalyst for unparalleled transformation. While automation can streamline operations and foster efficiency, it also prompts critical ethical questions about job security and privacy. Leaders must strike a balance between leveraging emergent tech to drive growth and ensuring that such advancements are inclusive and equitable. The convergence of AI and human ingenuity will not only reshape job roles but also demand new forms of collaboration and problem-solving. Consequently, organisations that invest in the ethical integration of these advancements, prioritise continuous learning, and cultivate a culture of innovation will emerge as frontrunners in this brave new world. Exploring these opportunities now will prepare us to harness the full potential of tomorrow's technologies, making the strategic foresight we develop today indispensable for sustainable success.

The AI Revolution: Opportunities and Challenges

The AI revolution stands poised to transform our workplaces, presenting both remarkable opportunities and formidable challenges. As AI technologies become more integrated into daily operations, organisations can expect a surge in efficiency and a drastic reduction in repetitive tasks. However, the flip side of this technological leap raises crucial questions about job security and ethical practices. Forward-thinking leaders must navigate this terrain with a balanced approach, fostering innovation while safeguarding their workforce's well-being. By embracing continuous learning and fostering a culture of adaptability, companies can not only harness AI's potential but also prepare Generation Alpha to thrive in this dynamic landscape. Ultimately, the goal is to create a future where technological advancements drive growth without compromising ethical standards or human value.

Integrating AI into Daily Operations has become a crucial strategy for businesses aiming to stay competitive and innovative. For forward-thinking leaders, HR professionals, and strategists, the challenge lies not just in adopting AI but embedding it seamlessly into the daily routines and processes of their organisations. This isn't merely about using AI as a tool; it's about transforming the very fabric of workplace operations to harness AI's full potential.

Let's start by understanding the scope of AI integration. AI isn't just for tech giants or highly specialised fields—it's applicable across sectors and scales. Small businesses and large corporations alike can benefit from AI's capabilities in automating repetitive tasks, providing deeper data insights, and enhancing customer interactions. The key is to identify the operational pain points that AI can alleviate and strategically implement solutions.

Automating routine tasks is one of the most immediate benefits of integrating AI into daily operations. Consider HR processes: AI can streamline tasks such as payroll processing, leave management, and even preliminary resume screening. By freeing up time spent on these routine tasks, employees can focus on more strategic, value-adding activities, thereby increasing overall productivity and job satisfaction.

Customer service is another area where AI integration shines. Chatbots and virtual assistants can handle a large volume of customer inquiries 24/7, providing quick and efficient responses. This not only improves customer satisfaction but also reduces the workload on human agents, allowing them to handle more complex queries. It's essential to ensure that these AI-driven interactions maintain a high level of personalisation to avoid the pitfalls of impersonal customer service.

Data analytics is perhaps where AI's impact is most profound. With AI, businesses can analyse vast amounts of data with unprecedented speed and accuracy. This capability powers better decision-making through predictive analytics, trend analysis, and personalised recommendations. For Generation Alpha, who will enter the workforce with an inherent affinity for technology, leveraging AI's data capabilities will be second nature and a baseline expectation.

However, merely introducing AI into the workplace isn't enough. Creating an environment where AI can thrive involves a cultural shift. Leaders must foster a culture of continuous learning and adaptability. Employees need to feel comfortable working alongside AI, understanding how to maximise its benefits, and seeing these technologies as partners rather than replacements.

Training and development play a pivotal role in this cultural shift. Employees at all levels should receive comprehensive training on the AI tools being introduced. This includes understanding how the technology works, the data it uses, and most importantly, how to interpret its outputs. When employees are well-equipped with this knowledge, they can make more informed decisions and contribute to the organisation's innovative potential.

Transparency in AI operations is another critical factor. Leaders must clearly communicate how AI technologies will be used, the benefits they bring, and the safeguards in place to protect employee and customer data. This transparency builds trust and encourages openness toward AI adoption. It also aligns with the ethical values and social responsibility that are core to Generation Alpha's mindset.

AI-driven decision-making is a powerful tool but must be approached with caution. It's essential to maintain a balance between AI recommendations and human judgment to avoid over-reliance on algorithms. By combining AI insights with human expertise, organisations can make more balanced and ethical decisions, reflecting a blend of efficiency and empathy.

The integration of AI should also focus on collaborative technologies. Tools that facilitate teamwork—such as AI-driven project management software or collaborative platforms embedded with intelligent features—can significantly enhance productivity. These platforms can optimise task allocation, predict project timelines, and even identify potential bottlenecks, ensuring smoother project execution.

Looking at the bigger picture, integrating AI into daily operations isn't just an optimisation strategy; it's a pathway to innovation. AI can uncover patterns and insights that might be invisible to the human eye, offering new avenues for product development, market strategies, and customer engagement. For forward-thinking organisations, AI becomes a catalyst for groundbreaking ideas and innovation.

Security and ethical considerations cannot be overlooked. As AI integration grows, so do the risks related to data privacy and security. Robust policies and practices must be in place to safeguard sensitive information. This includes regular audits, adherence to regulations, and transparent communication with stakeholders about how data is collected, used, and protected.

Aligning AI integration with the organisation's broader goals is vital. AI shouldn't be viewed as an isolated initiative but rather a part of the overall strategy. Whether it's driving sustainability efforts or enhancing operational efficiency, AI applications must resonate with the company's mission and values. This alignment ensures that AI integration supports long-term objectives and creates coherent value across the organisation.

Ultimately, successful AI integration is about creating symbiosis between technology and human capability. It's about recognising the strengths and limitations of both and designing workflows where they complement each other. This approach not only maximises the benefits of AI but also empowers employees, fostering a culture of continuous improvement and innovative thinking.

In conclusion, the journey to integrating AI into daily operations is multifaceted, requiring a balance of technology, people, and strategy. For forward-thinking leaders and HR professionals, the goal is to create a workplace where AI augments human potential, driving both efficiency and innovation. It's about preparing for a future where Generation Alpha's seamless interaction with technology sets new standards for what the workplace can achieve.

Ethical Considerations and Job Security must be at the forefront of our minds as we navigate the dramatic shifts that AI and automation are bringing to the workplace. It's crucial to remember that while technology can drive efficiency and innovation, it must also be balanced with our responsibilities as employers and stewards of the workforce. We can't simply adopt new technologies without considering the implications for job roles and employee well-being.

In recent years, the conversation around AI and automation has largely focused on the potential for job displacement. There's an underlying concern among workers about job security – a feeling that their roles may become redundant as machines and algorithms grow more capable. Therefore, addressing these fears transparently and proactively is key for forward-thinking leaders. Engaging in honest discussions about how technology will be employed and offering reassurance about plans to upskill or reassign affected employees can significantly mitigate anxiety.

The ethical deployment of AI in the workplace demands a nuanced approach. For instance, an algorithm that streamlines recruitment processes shouldn't inadvertently perpetuate biases. Similarly, automation in manufacturing must account for workers' safety and job transition plans. These examples underscore the importance of ethical oversight at every step of technology integration.

An essential strategy for maintaining job security while embracing automation is investment in continuous learning and development. By providing robust training programmes, companies can equip their employees with new skills that align with the evolving demands of their roles. This proactive approach not only fosters job security but also enhances overall productivity and innovation within the organisation.

Additionally, there's an ethical imperative to consider the broader societal impact of AI and automation. Leaders must weigh the benefits of efficiency against the potential for increased inequality. The deployment of technology should aim to elevate the workforce rather than exacerbate economic disparities. This aligns with Generation Alpha's core value of social responsibility and demands a balanced, thoughtful approach.

Integrating AI ethically means ensuring transparency in how decisions are made. Employees must understand the 'why' behind implementing new technologies. This transparency builds trust and helps demystify the changes underway, reducing resistance and fostering a collaborative environment. Trust is the bedrock upon which successful integration rests.

Companies might also consider establishing ethics committees to oversee technology deployment. These committees can ensure that the introduction of AI and automation adheres to a framework of fairness and responsibility, providing a safeguard against unintended consequences. By including diverse perspectives, these committees can better anticipate and address potential ethical issues.

The challenge of job security amid rapid technological change isn't solely a company issue; it's a societal one. Governments, educational institutions, and businesses must collaborate to create a resilient labour market. This includes advocating for policies that support retraining programmes and unemployment insurance reforms that can better assist displaced workers.

An often overlooked aspect is the emotional and psychological impact of job displacement. Leaders must recognise and address the stress and uncertainty that employees may face during transitions. Providing mental health support and fostering a compassionate workplace culture can significantly help employees navigate these changes.

Moreover, it's imperative to align technological advancements with the company's long-term vision and values. Short-term gains should never come at the expense of ethical considerations and employee well-being. Sustainable growth is based on a foundation of trust and mutual respect between employer and employee.

Tackling these challenges also presents an opportunity for brands to position themselves as ethical leaders. Demonstrating a commitment to job security and ethical use of technology can enhance a company's reputation and attract top talent. In the age of social media, where corporate actions are scrutinised like never before, such commitment can be a significant differentiator.

Future-proofing the workforce involves more than just adapting to change; it requires anticipating it. Companies must cultivate a forward-thinking mindset, continually assessing how emerging technologies can be integrated ethically and responsibly. This anticipatory approach is key to staying ahead of potential ethical dilemmas.

There's also a crucial role for mentorship in this evolving landscape. Seasoned professionals can guide younger employees through the complexities of technological change, fostering a culture of learning and resilience. This intergenerational collaboration can serve as a stabilising force during times of significant transition.

Ultimately, the ethical integration of AI and the assurance of job security aren't just about preserving roles; they're about honouring the human element of the workplace. Technology should enhance human capabilities and enable us to focus on what truly matters – creativity, problem-solving, and meaningful interpersonal interactions.

By approaching AI and automation with a balanced perspective, leaders can ensure that their organisations not only survive but thrive in this new era. The goal is to create a future where innovation and ethical considerations coexist harmoniously, benefiting employees, companies, and society as a whole.

Emerging Technologies: Shaping the Future of Work

The integration of emerging technologies is not just an evolution; it's a revolution reshaping the very fabric of the workplace. As we navigate the inevitable shift towards a digitally-driven environment, the rise of artificial intelligence, blockchain, and immersive realities like virtual and augmented reality are pivotal. These technologies don't merely augment our capabilities; they redefine them, making once-impossible tasks seamlessly achievable. For Generation Alpha, digital natives with an intrinsic understanding of technology, leveraging these advancements will be second nature. This creates unparalleled opportunities for innovation and efficiency but also necessitates a proactive approach to ethical considerations and job security. As forward-thinking leaders, HR professionals, and strategists, recognising and harnessing these technologies is essential. It's about crafting workplaces that are not only futuristic but adaptive, inclusive, and resilient to the rapidly changing landscape. By embracing these tools and fostering an environment ripe for continuous learning and flexibility, we can ensure that Generation Alpha thrives, bringing forth an era where sustainability and technological prowess go hand in hand.

Virtual Reality and Augmented Reality in Training have the potential to revolutionise how we approach workforce development. Generation Alpha, immersed in technology from their formative years, will expect training programmes that are not just informative but immersive. VR and AR, bridging the gap between theoretical knowledge and practical application, meet this expectation superbly. This presents a shift: training becomes a dynamic experience rather than a static obligation.

Traditional training methods often fall short in engaging employees, leading to suboptimal retention of information. Think about stale PowerPoint presentations and monotonous lectures. In contrast, VR and AR offer interactive simulations where employees can practice skills in a risk-free environment. They embody the 'learn by doing' philosophy. For instance, medical professionals can practise surgeries without any risk to patients, and engineers can assemble machinery in a virtual setup before touching actual hardware.

The effectiveness of these technologies isn't speculative. Studies have demonstrated that VR training can result in a 75% increase in learning retention. This is notably higher compared to traditional methods. AR can overlay critical information onto real-world objects, which can be particularly valuable in fields requiring precision, such as manufacturing or logistics. The implication here is profound:

investing in VR and AR is not just about adopting new tech; it's about fundamentally driving better learning outcomes.

Furthermore, the use of VR and AR can foster inclusivity and accessibility in training programmes. With these tools, we can easily adjust simulations to accommodate workers with disabilities or different learning styles. This flexibility extends beyond accessibility; it allows for tailored training experiences. A new hire might need comprehensive foundational training, while a seasoned employee might benefit from advanced skill reinforcement.

Given that Generation Alpha will likely have different learning preferences, the ability of VR and AR to provide personalised training paths becomes crucial. A call centre might, for instance, use VR to simulate challenging customer interactions. Agents can practice repeatedly until they master the necessary skills. This customisation not only enhances competence but also builds confidence. When employees feel competent and prepared, their productivity and job satisfaction naturally improve.

These technologies are also invaluable for bridging the gap between theoretical training and real-world experience. A crucial part of training is often the transition from learning to doing. In many industries, this gap is evident. VR and AR can act as a bridge, providing a safe space for employees to apply what they've learned before they encounter real-world consequences. Retail employees, for example, can simulate handling high-pressure sales scenarios or customer complaints in a virtual environment.

Moreover, the integration of VR and AR in training aligns perfectly with Generation Alpha's desire for continuous improvement and lifelong learning. These tools can easily be updated with the latest information, industry standards, or techniques, ensuring that training content remains relevant. Such dynamism is crucial in a rapidly changing world where the shelf life of skills is becoming increasingly short.

Another compelling benefit is cost efficiency. Initial investments in VR and AR infrastructures might seem high. However, the long-term savings can be substantial. Companies save on travel costs for in-person training, decrease ongoing material costs, and reduce the time employees spend off the job for training. Over time, these savings can be significant, particularly for large organisations.

The potential for global training is another aspect worth noting. With VR and AR, geographical boundaries dissolve. Companies with a global footprint can roll out uniform training programmes across all locations without logistical complications. Consistency in training ensures that all employees, regardless of location, receive the same high-quality education. This is particularly beneficial for maintaining brand and service standards.

Adoption of VR and AR in training also signals a company's forward-thinking stance. It's a strong message to Generation Alpha that the organisation is invested in cutting-edge technologies and values innovation. This can be a significant factor in attracting and retaining top talent from this tech-savvy generation. Companies not only convey that they are modern workplaces but also that they are committed to employee development.

In the context of soft skills training, VR and AR can provide scenarios to develop skills like leadership, teamwork, and conflict resolution. These are often difficult to teach through traditional methods. Immersive environments allow employees to experience complex social situations and practice their responses. This can be instrumental in building a more empathetic and collaborative workplace culture.

Let's not overlook the role of feedback. In VR and AR environments, feedback can be immediate and highly detailed. Imagine an employee navigating a virtual hazardous materials scenario. The system can instantly highlight mistakes, suggest improvements, and offer replay options. This kind of immediate feedback loop accelerates learning and rectifies errors before they become ingrained habits.

Moreover, the use of AI within VR and AR can further personalise the training experience. By analysing performance, the system can adjust the difficulty, offer additional resources, or suggest further areas for improvement. This hyper-personalisation ensures that employees are always learning at an optimal pace, tailored to their capabilities and needs.

In summary, integrating VR and AR into training initiatives is not merely about adopting new technologies for the sake of trendiness. It's about fundamentally enhancing how employees learn and apply their skills. For Generation Alpha, this approach aligns perfectly with their comfort with technology and their expectations for immersive, engaging learning experiences. As leaders and HR professionals, embracing VR and AR in training is a strategic move to ensure that our future workforce is not only prepared but also highly motivated and proficient.

Investing in these technologies is, in essence, investing in people. It demonstrates a commitment to their continuous growth and development, which in turn fosters loyalty and drives organisational success. The future of training is here, and it's virtual, augmented, and incredibly transformative.

The Blockchain for Transparency and Security is more than just a buzzword circulating around the tech scene; it represents a pivotal shift in how businesses can enhance transparency and security in their operations, especially as they prepare to integrate Generation Alpha into the workplace. Blockchain, in essence, offers a decentralised and immutable ledger system that records transactions or interactions in a way that is both transparent and secure. It's not just about protecting data; it's about fostering a new level of trust and accountability within the organisation.

Imagine a workplace where employee interactions, from contractual agreements to performance reviews, are recorded on a blockchain. This system eliminates the potential for miscommunication or manipulation of records. When Generation Alpha, a cohort known for their tech-savviness and demand for transparency, enters the workforce, they'll expect these kinds of advanced solutions to be in place. They won't just want a promise of integrity; they'll want proof of it.

Firstly, let's delve into transparency. In traditional workplaces, information flow often gets bottlenecked or skewed by hierarchical processes. Blockchain technology disrupts this by ensuring all recorded information is available to every stakeholder in real-time. This decentralisation means there's no single point of control or failure, which naturally appeals to Generation Alpha's values of inclusivity and fairness. When they see an organisation where data flows freely and transparently, they're more likely to trust and invest their energy.

Security, on the other hand, has become a paramount concern in the digital age. With cyber-attacks and data breaches becoming more frequent, businesses can't afford to be careless. Blockchain's cryptographic nature makes it incredibly secure. Every block in the chain contains a cryptographic hash of the previous block, a timestamp, and transaction data. Altering any part of the chain is practically impossible without majority consensus, providing a robust defense against tampering.

Generation Alpha has grown up amid unprecedented levels of data breaches and online threats. As they step into the professional world, their expectations around data security will be non-negotiable.

Companies that utilise blockchain technology can offer this security with unprecedented reliability. They can ensure that sensitive information, whether related to HR records, financial transactions, or client data, is handled with the utmost care.

Blockchain's capacity for fostering accountability further aligns with Generation Alpha's value system. In a blockchain-based workflow, every action is recorded and time-stamped. This transparency doesn't just provide a clear record; it promotes a culture of accountability. Employees know that their actions are logged and can be audited, which can significantly reduce unethical behaviour. This level of accountability resonates particularly well with a generation that has been brought up to value integrity and transparency.

That's not all. Blockchain can also revolutionise the way contracts are managed within the workplace. Known as smart contracts, these are self-executing contracts with the terms directly written into code. They automatically enforce and verify the terms of a contract, reducing the need for intermediaries and drastically cutting down on delays and disputes. For a generation used to immediate and seamless digital interactions, smart contracts streamline administrative processes and align perfectly with their expectations for efficiency.

A practical illustration of blockchain's role could be in tracking and verifying the credentials and professional achievements of employees. Traditional methods often involve cumbersome paperwork and can be prone to forgery. A blockchain ledger, however, provides a verified and unalterable record of an employee's qualifications and work history. This not only speeds up the recruiting process but also enhances trust between employer and employee.

Blockchain's utility in performance management should not be underestimated. Imagine performance reviews that are completely transparent, tamper-proof, and available for both the employee and management to review at any time. This could dismantle biases and subjective evaluations that often plague traditional performance appraisal systems. By aligning reviews with transparent metrics recorded on a blockchain, organisations can ensure a more fair and objective evaluation process, which is crucial for motivating Generation Alpha.

Moreover, the integration of blockchain can stretch beyond internal operations to customer interactions, which is indirectly relevant to the workplace environment Gen Alpha will thrive in. For instance, supply chain transparency can be significantly enhanced through blockchain. Companies can transparently share the source of their materials or the location of production, thereby aligning with the social responsibility values highly regarded by Generation Alpha.

In terms of *data privacy*, blockchain technology stands on solid ground. Unlike traditional databases that store data in one central place, blockchain distributes this information across multiple nodes. This means that there isn't a single point of vulnerability. For Generation Alpha, who are aware of the implications of data misuse, this decentralised nature of blockchain offers a more trustworthy approach to managing personal and sensitive information.

For fostering a collaborative and innovative culture, blockchain can serve as a foundation for numerous applications. Take for instance, the implementation of decentralised autonomous organisations (DAOs), where governance is conducted through smart contracts and decision-making is transparent and shared among stakeholders. This participative and decentralised form of governance can be incredibly appealing to Generation Alpha, who value inclusive and democratic systems.

Furthermore, the adaptability of blockchain technology allows for seamless integration with other emerging technologies such as AI and IoT, forming a strong backbone for innovative uses. The capability to store and process vast amounts of data securely and transparently also means that organisations can pursue ambitious tech-driven projects without compromising on integrity or security. This aligns with Generation Alpha's expectation for workplaces that are not just technologically advanced but also ethically sound.

Organisations that fail to adopt such robust and forward-thinking technologies may find themselves lagging in the competition for top Gen Alpha talent. This generation is highly discerning and will gravitate towards companies that embody the ethical, transparent, and secure frameworks they were brought up to value. Therefore, embracing blockchain isn't just a strategic advantage; it's becoming a business imperative.

Ultimately, the implementation of blockchain technology represents a commitment to the values of transparency, security, and innovation. These are not just technicalities; they are fundamental principles that can significantly enhance workplace culture and efficiency. As businesses prepare to welcome Generation Alpha into their ranks, the strategic adoption of blockchain could very well be the differentiator that propels them into a future where trust, accountability, and innovation thrive.

Chapter 4:
New Leadership Paradigms

As organisations prepare for the influx of Generation Alpha into the workforce, it becomes increasingly clear that traditional leadership models must evolve. The hierarchical structures that once defined corporate environments are giving way to more fluid and adaptable frameworks. Leaders will need to exhibit a higher level of emotional intelligence, embracing empathy to connect genuinely with their teams. This up-and-coming generation values transparency and inclusivity, and expects a leadership style that is more collaborative and less authoritative. The future's most successful leaders will be those who inspire innovation by creating safe spaces for risk-taking and learning from failure. Rewarding creativity and recognising individual contributions will foster a culture where ideas flourish, and adaptability reigns. It isn't just about guiding a team through tasks anymore; it's about nurturing an environment where everyone feels valued and empowered to drive change. By embracing these new paradigms, leaders can steer their organisations towards a future defined by resilience, agility, and perpetual growth.

Leading Generation Alpha: Adaptability and Empathy

In leading Generation Alpha, adaptability and empathy aren't just buzzwords—they're essential leadership traits. This generation, having grown up in a digital world where change is rapid and constant, expects leaders to be flexible and responsive. To foster an environment where Generation Alpha can thrive, leaders must demonstrate an authentic understanding of their unique perspectives and needs. Adaptability means not only embracing technological advancements but also anticipating shifts in workforce dynamics and cultural norms. Empathy, on the other hand, involves actively listening and valuing the emotional well-being of younger employees. When leaders intertwine these qualities, they create a culture that is resilient, inclusive, and primed for innovation. The result is a harmonious workplace where Generation Alpha feels understood and empowered to contribute their best ideas, ensuring long-term success and mutual growth.

From Hierarchies to Networks: A Shift in Power Dynamics encapsulates one of the most profound transformations occurring in modern organisations. Generation Alpha, with their distinct set of values and expectations, is leading a movement away from rigid, top-down structures towards more fluid and interconnected systems. This shift is not just a change in organisational charts; it's a revolution in how power is distributed, decisions are made, and collaboration happens across various levels of the workplace.

Traditional hierarchies have long been the backbone of corporate structures. They provide clear lines of authority and responsibility, facilitating efficient management and control. However, these systems can also stifle creativity, impede swift decision-making, and create a chasm between leadership and the workforce. Enter Generation Alpha, who, raised in an era of rapid technological advancement and social media connectivity, naturally gravitate towards networked forms of organisation.

Networks function through nodes and connections, reflecting the digital ecosystems that Generation Alpha navigates with ease. In a networked organisation, information flows more freely, collaboration thrives through informal yet effective channels, and innovation is sparked from various sources rather than trickling down from the top. For forward-thinking leaders, recognising and fostering these characteristics is crucial.

So, what does this shift mean for leadership dynamics? Leadership in networked environments demands a balance between authority and empowerment. Leaders must act more like facilitators, providing the resources and guidance that enable employees to self-organise and collaborate efficiently. Empathy and adaptability become cornerstones of leadership as the generational shift towards networks progresses.

In practical terms, this shift can significantly impact decision-making processes. Traditional hierarchies often involve lengthy chains of approval, but a networked approach allows for more autonomy and faster decision-making. Employees equipped with the right tools and trust can respond in real-time, making the organisation more agile and responsive to external changes. This form of empowerment is particularly appealing to Generation Alpha, who value immediacy and influence in their work.

Leadership is no longer about maintaining control over subordinates; it's about orchestrating an environment where every individual feels valued and influential. By embracing this mindset, organisations can spur greater engagement and productivity, aspects that are paramount for retaining Generation Alpha talent. These young professionals are looking for workplaces where their input is encouraged, and their potential is fully realised.

Generation Alpha also brings a strong inclination towards collaboration. Raised on platforms that thrive on peer-to-peer interaction, they expect the same level of openness and connectivity in their professional lives. Hierarchies often isolate departments and create silos, but networked structures break down these barriers, fostering cross-functional teams that can tackle complex problems together.

Organisations must invest in tools and platforms that facilitate this new way of working. Collaboration software, instant messaging, and cloud-based solutions play a critical role in ensuring that teams, regardless of their location, remain connected and efficient. For Generation Alpha, who has grown up with smartphones and social networks, leveraging these tools comes naturally. It's not just about the tools, though; the organisational culture must promote and reward collaborative efforts.

Moreover, the shift towards networks aligns seamlessly with the values of transparency and inclusivity that Generation Alpha holds dear. In a networked structure, transparency is not just a buzzword but a practical necessity. Open communication channels and shared access to information ensure that everyone, regardless of their position, is in the loop. This kind of environment builds trust and reinforces a sense of community, crucial for high morale and low turnover rates.

Inclusivity also gets a significant boost in networked organisations. Traditional hierarchies often perpetuate biases and favouritism, but a networked approach levels the playing field, enabling a more diverse array of voices to be heard. An inclusive environment where diverse perspectives are not just tolerated but celebrated can lead to groundbreaking innovations and a richer workplace culture.

Another critical aspect of this shift is the way it promotes continuous learning and adaptability. In a network, the speed of change and information flow necessitates that employees constantly update their skills and knowledge. Lifelong learning becomes embedded in the organisational DNA, setting Generation Alpha up for success in a rapidly evolving job market. Leaders can harness this by providing ample opportunities for professional development and encouraging a mindset of perpetual growth.

For HR professionals and strategists, accommodating this shift involves rethinking traditional talent management practices.

Recruitment, onboarding, and retention strategies must align with the expectations of a networked workplace. Emphasising roles that allow for autonomy, creativity, and collaboration will attract top Generation Alpha talent. Performance assessments should also evolve to value contributions within a network, looking at how employees add to the collective intelligence and success of the organisation.

As we transition from hierarchies to networks, it is essential to remember that this shift is not about dismantling all forms of structure. Instead, it's about achieving a balance where structure serves as a support, not a constraint. Networked organisations require clear objectives and accountability, but within a framework that allows for flexibility and resilience.

In conclusion, the move from hierarchies to networks is not just a structural change—it's a cultural transformation. Generation Alpha, with their distinctive approach to technology and collaboration, is the catalyst driving this shift. For leaders willing to embrace this new paradigm, the rewards are immense: increased innovation, speed, and employee satisfaction. The future of work is interconnected and dynamic, so organisations must adapt to thrive in this new era. The time to start is now, and the path forward is through networks, not hierarchies.

Emotional Intelligence: A Key Leadership Trait has never been more vital than in today's rapidly evolving workplace. With Generation Alpha set to enter the workforce, the traditional models of leadership will require significant adaptation. Emotional Intelligence (EI) can act as the catalyst for this change, bridging the gap between conventional management styles and the empathetic, flexible approach necessary for the future.

For forward-thinking leaders, understanding the value of EI is paramount. At its core, emotional intelligence involves self-awareness, self-regulation, empathy, social skills, and motivation. When leaders exhibit these traits, they're better equipped to manage diverse teams, navigate complex emotional landscapes, and foster a culture of innovation and inclusivity.

Generation Alpha will demand more from their workplaces than any previous generation. Raised in an era of constant connectivity, they'll expect real-time feedback, transparent communication, and authentic relationships. Leaders with high EI will be essential in meeting these expectations, creating an environment where young talent feels valued and understood.

Understanding and managing one's own emotions is the first step to EI. For leaders, this means being aware of their emotional triggers and responses. It's not just about staying calm under pressure; it's about recognising stressors early and employing strategies to mitigate their impact. A leader who practices self-regulation can maintain an atmosphere of stability and reassurance, even during turbulent times.

The ability to understand and manage others' emotions – empathy – is equally critical. Leaders who can put themselves in their employees' shoes will be more adept at addressing concerns, fostering a sense of belonging, and facilitating open communication. This is particularly important for Generation Alpha, who value authenticity and honest interaction above hierarchical formalities.

Social skills are another cornerstone of EI. Strong leaders don't just instruct; they connect. They build networks and create synergies that drive collective success. For Generation Alpha, accustomed to the collaborative nature of social media and online communities, a leader who excels in social interaction can bridge the divide between digital fluency and workplace productivity.

The role of motivation in EI can't be overlooked. It's not just about inspiring others; it's about having a genuine passion for the work and a commitment to achieving goals. Leaders who demonstrate intrinsic motivation not only inspire their teams but also build a culture where innovation and perseverance are the norms. For Generation Alpha, a motivated leader exemplifies a career path worth aspiring to.

EI-oriented leaders excel in conflict resolution. By recognising and addressing underlying emotional issues, they can navigate disputes more effectively, leading to quicker resolutions and a more harmonious work environment. As Generation Alpha enters the workforce, they'll bring with them diverse perspectives and backgrounds, increasing the potential for conflict but also the opportunity for enriched, multifaceted problem-solving.

Furthermore, emotional intelligence supports the creation of psychologically safe workplaces. Employees who feel emotionally secure are more likely to speak up, share ideas, and take calculated risks. This atmosphere of trust is particularly important for Generation Alpha, who are generally more socially conscious and attuned to issues of mental health and well-being.

Effective feedback is another area where EI shines. Traditional feedback methods may not resonate with Generation Alpha's need for continuous, real-time input. Emotionally intelligent leaders tailor their feedback to be constructive and empathetic, helping their teams grow without feeling demoralised. This approach encourages a growth mindset, essential for personal and professional development.

Incorporating EI into leadership also drives engagement. Leaders who are attuned to the emotional undercurrents within their teams can take proactive measures to boost morale and maintain high levels of engagement. For a generation that thrives on instant gratification and connection, this kind of responsive leadership can make all the difference.

Resilience is another attribute closely linked to EI. Leaders who demonstrate resilience in the face of adversity set a powerful example for their teams. They show that setbacks are temporary and surmountable, fostering an environment where failure is viewed as a stepping stone to success. This resilience will be crucial as Generation Alpha navigates the uncertainties of a rapidly changing job market.

Leaders with high EI are better at recognising potential in their team members. They see beyond the resume and tap into the unique strengths and passions of each individual. For Generation Alpha, who value personalisation and authenticity, this approach can significantly enhance job satisfaction and retention.

Ultimately, integrating emotional intelligence into leadership practices doesn't just benefit the individual leader; it transforms the entire organisational culture. It paves the way for a more compassionate, creative, and collaborative workplace, aligning perfectly with the values and expectations of Generation Alpha.

So, as we prepare to welcome this new generation into the workforce, let's focus on cultivating our own emotional intelligence. It's not merely a leadership trait; it's the foundation for a thriving, dynamic, and adaptive workplace. Through EI, we can create an environment where every employee, regardless of generation, can truly flourish.

Cultivating a Culture of Innovation

To foster a culture of innovation, leaders must create environments that not only welcome fresh ideas but actively encourage calculated risks and embrace diverse viewpoints. In these forward-thinking workplaces, Generation Alpha's inherent affinity for technology and creativity can be leveraged to ignite a newfound era of ingenuity. It's not just about celebrating successful innovations; it's about valuing the learning journey, even when it includes failures. Establishing a workplace where questioning the status quo is the norm rather than the exception underscores the importance of continuous improvement. Leaders can drive this by championing transparency, promoting cross-functional collaboration, and providing opportunities for employees to pursue passion projects. By embedding these principles into the organisational fabric, companies can remain agile and responsive to the inevitable changes on the horizon, ensuring they stay ahead of the curve and maintain a competitive edge in an ever-evolving marketplace.

Encouraging Risk-Taking and Learning from Failure are twin engines that drive innovation. Generation Alpha, with their innate tech-savviness and strong sense of social responsibility, are poised to be potent innovators. However, for them to flourish, today's leaders must cultivate an environment where taking risks is not just tolerated but encouraged. We must reframe the narrative around failure, perceiving it not as the end of a journey but as a crucial step towards success.

One key to encouraging risk-taking is to ensure psychological safety within teams. When employees feel safe to voice their ideas, without the fear of ridicule or harsh repercussions, they become more willing to step out of their comfort zones. A study by Google's Project Aristotle highlighted that psychological safety is the number one factor for a successful team. Leaders must foster a culture where questioning the status quo and proposing bold ideas are met with intrigue and support.

Generation Alpha's upbringing in a digital, rapidly changing world means they are more accustomed to taking risks than previous generations. This generation's approach to learning is iterative, often involving quick experimentation, failure, and adjustment. Leaders should harness this iterative approach by creating processes that allow for rapid prototyping and agile development. This means not only accepting but celebrating small failures as evidence of progress.

Structured opportunities for risk-taking can also be instrumental. Implementing innovation labs or 'failure funds' can give employees dedicated spaces and resources to experiment. These environments should be free from the usual performance metrics and goal pressures, providing a sandbox where creativity can thrive. Leaders should clearly articulate that the goal is exploration and learning, not immediate success.

Learning from Failure

Encouraging risk-taking only becomes fruitful when paired with a robust mechanism for learning from failures. Leaders must instil a mindset that sees failure as data – valuable insights on what doesn't work and why. Post-mortem analyses and after-action reviews can be useful tools for dissecting failures constructively. These reviews should focus on understanding the root causes and deriving actionable lessons, rather than assigning blame.

Additionally, transparent sharing of these lessons can benefit the entire organisation. Creating an internal knowledge base or learning repository where teams can document their experiments and outcomes helps build a reservoir of collective intelligence. When Generation Alpha employees see a pattern of failures turned into learning opportunities, they are more likely to embrace their own failures.

Storytelling can also play a vital role. Sharing stories of well-known failures that eventually led to groundbreaking successes can inspire and motivate. Icons such as Thomas Edison, who famously took thousands of attempts before perfecting the light bulb, or modern-day entrepreneurs like Elon Musk, who have faced public failures before achieving their visions, serve as powerful reminders that failure is often a precursor to success.

Another aspect is mentorship and peer support. Experienced mentors can provide guidance and perspective to younger employees, helping them navigate failures more effectively. Peer support groups or 'fail clubs' where employees come together to share their experiences of failure can reduce the stigma and reinforce a culture of mutual learning.

It's also crucial that leaders lead by example. When leaders openly admit their own mistakes and share the lessons derived from them, it humanises them and sets a powerful precedent. This transparency can help break down silos and foster a culture where experimentation is not just top-down but ingrained at every level of the organisation.

Rewarding risk-taking is another powerful lever. Recognise and incentivise not just the successes but the attempts. Performance appraisal systems and reward mechanisms should reflect an appreciation for innovative efforts, regardless of the outcome. Celebrating risk-takers reinforces the message that the organisation values innovation and is committed to exploring new frontiers.

Integrating New Practices

Integrating these practices requires a commitment to cultural transformation. Leaders must actively communicate the vision and values that underscore the importance of risk-taking and learning from failure. Embedding these values into the organisational DNA can be achieved through regular training, workshops, and continuous communication efforts. Internal communications like newsletters, town halls, and intranet updates can regularly spotlight examples of risk-taking and the learnings derived from failures.

Embedding a feedback mechanism is key. Regular feedback loops where employees can voice their thoughts on risk-taking initiatives help refine these efforts. This dialogue ensures that the strategies remain dynamic and responsive to employee needs and organisational goals. Feedback also signals that leadership is attentive and committed to fostering a genuinely innovative culture.

Change is never easy, and there will inevitably be resistance. Addressing this requires patience, empathy, and persistence. Leaders must be prepared to tackle scepticism and encourage a shift in mindset through consistent, small wins that showcase the benefits of embracing risk and learning from failure.

Measuring the impact of these efforts is equally important. Leaders should establish key performance indicators (KPIs) that reflect innovation metrics, such as the number of new ideas generated, time to market for new initiatives, and cross-departmental collaboration rates. Regularly reviewing these KPIs will help in fine-tuning the strategies and demonstrating the tangible benefits of a culture that encourages risk-taking.

In conclusion, **Encouraging Risk-Taking and Learning from Failure** is not an auxiliary activity but a central pillar of an innovative workplace. For Generation Alpha, who are natural experimenters, this approach resonates deeply with their ethos. By championing risk-taking and reframing failure as a learning tool, today's leaders can unlock incredible potential, driving their organisations towards unprecedented innovation and growth. Let's commit to this transformative journey and prepare our workplaces for a future where bold ideas flourish and learning from failure becomes a powerful catalyst for success.

Reward Systems and Recognition for Innovation have always been pivotal in driving a culture of creativity and continuous improvement. However, with Generation Alpha entering the workplace, traditional approaches may need a rethink. This generation, raised amidst rapid technological advancements and an emphasis on social responsibility, values more than just monetary rewards.

To inspire and sustain innovation among Generation Alpha, it's crucial to develop reward systems that weave in elements of personal growth, purpose, and social impact. While monetary incentives still hold value, this group is likely to be more motivated by opportunities for learning, the chance to work on meaningful projects, and recognition that resonates on a personal level.

Innovation thrives in environments where experimentation is encouraged and failure is seen as a stepping stone to success. It's vital for leaders to cultivate such cultures by implementing reward systems that recognise not just the end products of innovation but also the process. This means celebrating incremental improvements, risk-taking, and even the insights gained from failed attempts.

Generation Alpha is inherently collaborative, having grown up with social media and online communities. Therefore, reward systems that highlight team achievements can be particularly effective. Offering group rewards, like team-building retreats or collaborative project showcases, can reinforce the importance of working together and spark further collective creativity.

Individual recognition doesn't need to feel impersonal. Personalised feedback and customised rewards can make a huge difference. It could be as simple as a personalised message from leadership appreciating an employee's innovative contribution or a tailored professional development opportunity that aligns with their career aspirations.

Public recognition can also be a powerful motivator. Whether it's through company-wide meetings, newsletters, or social media platforms, acknowledging innovative contributions publicly can boost morale and set a precedent for what the organisation values. Highlighting these achievements not only recognises the individual but also sets a benchmark for peers.

Additionally, integrating social and environmental impact into the reward systems resonates well with Generation Alpha. Rewards that include community service opportunities or contributions to sustainability projects can align employees' personal values with their professional efforts, fostering a deeper sense of purpose and engagement.

Award ceremonies and innovation competitions can serve as both recognition and motivation tools. Hosting events where innovative ideas are showcased and celebrated can create a sense of excitement and healthy competition. These events can also be opportunities for cross-departmental interactions, enriching the organisational culture.

Digital badges and gamification elements can add a layer of fun and engagement. Implementing systems where employees earn badges for innovative efforts, which can be displayed on internal profiles or used as part of a gamified reward system, can make the process of achieving recognition more interactive and enjoyable.

Transparency in how rewards are allocated is crucial. Generation Alpha values fairness and accountability. Clear criteria and processes for earning rewards can prevent any feelings of bias or favoritism and ensure that everyone feels equally motivated and recognised for their efforts.

Peer recognition systems can empower employees to recognise each other's contributions. Platforms that allow team members to highlight their peers' innovative ideas can foster a supportive environment. Peer recognition often feels more genuine and can strengthen team dynamics, leading to a more cohesive and innovative workplace.

Moreover, incorporating regular feedback loops where employees can voice their opinions on reward systems can ensure these systems remain relevant and effective. Listening to their feedback and making adjustments based on their input can demonstrate that the organisation values their contributions and is committed to creating an environment where they can thrive.

Ultimately, the goal of any reward system is to align organisational goals with personal motivations. By understanding what drives Generation Alpha and integrating those elements into the reward framework, organisations can foster and sustain a culture of innovation that benefits everyone. It's about creating an ecosystem where creativity is both recognised and rewarded in a manner that feels authentic and meaningful to the newest generation entering the workforce.

As Generation Alpha becomes an integral part of the workforce, the need for adaptive and thoughtful reward systems will only grow. Embracing this change proactively will not only attract and retain top talent but will also position organisations as leaders in innovation and employee satisfaction.

Chapter 5:
Education and Continuous Learning

In a world that's evolving at a breakneck speed, the importance of education and continuous learning can't be overstated. Generation Alpha, with its tech-savvy nature, needs more than traditional education to thrive. We must equip them with skills that extend beyond STEM, encompassing soft skills like communication, creativity, and critical thinking. The future workspace will demand professionals who are not just problem solvers but innovators, adept at navigating complex scenarios. Microlearning and online platforms will play pivotal roles in this transformation, offering flexible, just-in-time learning opportunities. It's crucial for employers to foster a culture of lifelong learning, encouraging employees to stay relevant in a rapidly changing world. The onus is on businesses to support continuous education and provide resources that promote growth, ensuring that their workforce remains agile and capable of meeting future demands. In essence, the future belongs to those who are willing to adapt, learn, and evolve continuously.

Preparing for the Future: Skills and Competencies

Preparing Generation Alpha for the future means investing in their development across a range of skills and competencies essential for tomorrow's dynamic workforce. As automation and AI reshape job landscapes, STEM education is crucial, but we can't overlook the importance of soft skills like communication, creativity, and critical thinking. These future leaders will navigate complex, technology-driven environments, and they'll need to be flexible and innovative problem solvers. Emphasising continuous learning—through methods like microlearning and online platforms—ensures they stay relevant in evolving industries. Employers play a pivotal role by offering training opportunities and fostering a culture of lifelong learning, enabling Gen Alpha to thrive and drive sustainability, adaptability, and innovation in the workplace. This comprehensive skillset will empower them to face challenges with confidence and make meaningful contributions to their organisations and society at large.

STEM and Beyond: A Broad Curriculum encapsulates the holistic approach that Generation Alpha will bring to the table as they enter the workforce. This is not just about accumulating technical skills; it's about preparing for a world that demands adaptability, creativity, and a keen understanding of diverse academic disciplines. Gone are the days when mastering maths and science alone would suffice. Today's forward-thinking organisations must acknowledge that a broad and inclusive curriculum is the bedrock of future success.

Emphasising a diversified curriculum means recognising the confluence of various subjects, which can collectively foster a more innovative and flexible workforce. While STEM (Science, Technology, Engineering, and Mathematics) remains fundamental, incorporating arts, humanities, and social sciences enriches problem-solving perspectives. Generation Alpha, having grown up with unprecedented access to information and multidimensional learning tools, will expect their education—and future employers—to take a similarly broad approach.

Imagine a young professional who doesn't just understand the algorithms behind artificial intelligence but can also discuss the ethical implications of AI usage. This holistic knowledge doesn't form in a vacuum; it's cultivated through a comprehensive educational framework that merges technical prowess with critical thinking and ethical reasoning. Such a well-rounded education resounds in Generation Alpha's values and will be indispensable in navigating the multifaceted challenges of the contemporary workplace.

Therefore, businesses aiming to integrate Generation Alpha successfully need to mirror this broad curriculum approach in their training and development programmes. No longer can employee training be restricted to job-specific skills. Forward-thinking leaders must invest in continuous learning ecosystems that encourage a blend of technical, creative, and social skills. In doing so, they're not just preparing employees for their current roles but future-proofing the organisation against shifts in the global economy and technological advancements.

Moreover, the integration of such a broad curriculum in the professional sphere must be underpinned by a commitment to lifelong learning. Generation Alpha is expected to be characterised by a continual desire to upskill, reflecting the dynamic nature of their early education. Employers should thus facilitate environments that offer diverse learning opportunities, from online courses and workshops to real-world problem-solving projects that require interdisciplinary approaches.

In practical terms, this means leveraging various educational platforms and methodologies. For example, microlearning, where information is broken down into bite-sized, manageable pieces, aligns perfectly with Generation Alpha's learning habits. These shorter, focused bursts of information can also facilitate the balancing act between work responsibilities and ongoing education—a challenge many professionals face today.

Another crucial aspect of integrating a broad curriculum lies in company culture. Organisations must encourage a culture where learning and curiosity are celebrated. This might involve establishing formal Learning and Development (L&D) departments tasked with implementing comprehensive training programmes that span across multiple disciplines. They could also incentivise employees to attend conferences, participate in cross-departmental projects, or even engage in volunteer work that broadens their perspectives and skill sets.

Furthermore, pairing traditional STEM subjects with arts and humanities encourages creative problem-solving and innovative thinking. For instance, an engineer with a background in the arts may approach a technical challenge with a unique perspective, offering solutions grounded in both practicality and creativity. It's this inter-section that often leads to groundbreaking innovations, as seen in fields like design thinking and human-computer interaction.

Internally, leadership must embody and champion this integrated approach, serving as role models for continuous, broad-based learning. Leaders could host "lunch and learn" sessions, discussing the latest trends in technology alongside ethical questions or societal impacts. Such initiatives not only build knowledge but also foster an inclusive and supportive workplace culture that values diverse intellectual contributions.

Equally important are collaborations and partnerships with educational institutions. Businesses should actively engage with schools, colleges, and universities to help shape curricula that reflect real-world demands and future trends. By providing insight into industry needs and technological advancements, companies can ensure that the next generation is not only technically proficient but holistically prepared for the workforce.

A broad curriculum also eliminates silos within organisations. When employees are versed in a variety of disciplines, they can communicate more effectively across departments, leading to better collaboration and innovation. Imagine a marketing team that understands data analytics or an IT department fluent in customer experience principles. Such cross-functional knowledge can transform how an organisation operates, making it more agile and responsive to market changes.

Let's not forget the international dimension. In our increasingly globalised world, understanding different cultures, global economics, and international regulations is vital. Generation Alpha's education is already shaped by this global perspective, given their early exposure to worldwide information networks. Businesses must continue this trend by offering training that includes international case studies and encourages cross-cultural competencies.

The impact on leadership strategies is significant too. Leaders must be prepared to guide teams where members have broad and varied educational backgrounds. This demands adaptability, empathy, and a willingness to continuously update their knowledge. Only then can they effectively harness the diverse talents within their teams, driving innovation and achieving organisational goals.

Lastly, a broad curriculum nurtures intrinsic motivation among employees. When individuals see the relevance of their learning to broader existential and societal questions, they're more likely to engage deeply and passionately with their work. This sense of purpose, a critical trait for motivating Generation Alpha, can translate into higher job satisfaction, better performance, and greater organisational loyalty.

In sum, embracing a broad curriculum isn't just an educational philosophy; it's a business imperative. It prepares individuals not only to meet current job requirements but to thrive in an ever-evolving world. By fostering a culture grounded in diverse learning and interdisciplinary approaches, organisations can unleash the full potential of Generation Alpha, spearheading innovation, adaptability, and sustainability in the workplace.

Soft Skills: Communication, Creativity, and Critical Thinking are the trifecta that will define the future workplace. As companies seek to integrate Generation Alpha, the nature of these skills and how they're cultivated will be pivotal. Let's delve into how these foundational competencies will shape the professional landscape and what leaders can do to nurture them.

Communication, at its core, is more complex than a simple exchange of words. With Generation Alpha, reared in a digital environment where communication modalities are ever-evolving, we must anticipate a shift. Traditional face-to-face interactions won't disappear, but they'll be supplemented with a range of digital communications. Messaging platforms, video calls, and perhaps even virtual reality meetings may become the norm.

One significant transformation for leaders and HR professionals to consider is the way Generation Alpha interacts. Raised on instant messaging, social media, and livestreams, their communication is immediate and often informal. Understanding and adapting to this rapid, casual style will be critical. Employers must balance it with the need for clear, concise, and formal communication in certain scenarios.

Furthermore, inclusive communication will be paramount. Generation Alpha, with its globally connected upbringing, values diversity and inclusivity in the workplace. Leaders must foster an environment where every voice is heard, ensuring that communication is not just top-down but also peer-to-peer across diverse teams. This inclusivity also demands sensitivity to cultural nuances and a keen awareness of avoiding biases in everyday discourse.

Shifting gears to creativity, Generation Alpha's world has been an immersive blend of reality and fiction, courtesy of video games, virtual reality, and augmented reality. This exposure has made them not only adept at thinking outside the box but also at dismantling the box entirely. Creativity for them is not an occasional burst of inspiration;

it's a continuous process embedded in their way of thinking and working.

Organisations can harness this boundless creativity by providing platforms for experimentation. Leaders should encourage new ideas and innovative thinking by creating a safe space where employees are not afraid to fail. Celebrating small wins and learning from setbacks will be essential in nurturing a creative culture. It's about shifting from a risk-averse attitude to one that sees experimentation as a pathway to improvement.

Drawing on creativity, problem-solving too will take a new dimension. Generation Alpha's approach will be more holistic, integrating technology and data seamlessly. Leaders who provide them with the right tools and technologies will see a surge in ingenious solutions. Think of AI-enhanced brainstorming sessions or leveraging big data for creative insights. The symbiosis of technology and creativity will define the future workplace's innovative capacity.

Critical thinking will underpin their ability to navigate the complex digital landscape. Growing up with abundant information, Generation Alpha has developed a knack for filtering and analysing data swiftly. However, the challenge lies in fostering deeper critical thinking that goes beyond skimming headlines or trending topics. Companies must invest in developing these analytical skills further.

Training programmes focused on critical thinking should encourage questioning assumptions, evaluating evidence, and synthesizing information from various sources. Leaders can model this behaviour by engaging in open discussions, presenting real-world problems for analysis, and challenging employees to provide evidence-based solutions. This continuous practice will help Generation Alpha sharpen their analytical acumen.

Moreover, ethical decision-making should be intertwined with critical thinking. In an age where misinformation can spread rapidly, the ability to discern fact from fiction and make morally sound decisions will be a vital skill. Equipping Generation Alpha with frameworks for ethical reasoning will ensure that they don't just solve problems effectively but also responsibly.

A fusion of these skills—communication, creativity, and critical thinking—forms a robust foundation for leadership development. Leaders themselves must exemplify these qualities, demonstrating adaptive communication styles, fostering an innovative environment, and leading with a critical eye. This modelling behaviour will cascade down, creating a culture where these soft skills are not just valued but practised daily.

Organisations looking to thrive in the coming decades will need to integrate ongoing training and development opportunities focused on these areas. This may involve workshops, mentorship programmes, and cross-disciplinary projects that encourage employees to step out of their comfort zones and apply these skills in diverse contexts. Continuous learning should be embedded in the company's fabric to keep pace with evolving competencies.

Another crucial aspect is technology's role in enhancing these soft skills. Leveraging digital tools to facilitate better communication, stimulate creativity through collaborative platforms, and enhance critical thinking via data analysis software will be essential. Technology should be seen as an enabler, helping to refine and amplify these inherent capabilities within Generation Alpha.

In conclusion, the integration of Generation Alpha into the workplace mandates a proactive approach to nurturing their soft skills. By focusing on adaptable communication, fostering an environment ripe for creativity, and sharpening critical thinking, companies can harness the full potential of this dynamic generation. Leadership in the future workplace will hinge on these skills, driving both individual and organisational success. Let this be a call to action for forward-thinking leaders to invest in these areas robustly.

Lifelong Learning: Staying Relevant in a Rapidly Changing World

In the fast-paced, ever-evolving landscape that is the modern workplace, the ability to continually learn and adapt is paramount. Lifelong learning isn't just about acquiring new skills—it's a mindset that prepares both individuals and organisations to thrive amid constant change. Generation Alpha, digital natives born into a world where information is just a click away, will expect an environment that fosters continuous self-improvement and innovation. As leaders and HR professionals, it's crucial to build a culture where ongoing education is not only encouraged but also seamlessly integrated into daily operations. This is the new standard for staying relevant. By investing in microlearning opportunities and leveraging online platforms, we can provide employees with the tools they need to keep their skills sharp and their minds agile. The emphasis shouldn't merely be on technical expertise; soft skills like creativity, critical thinking, and effective communication are equally vital. This approach not only upskills the workforce but also embeds a culture of resilience and adaptability that will drive your organisation forward in an uncertain world.

Microlearning and Online Platforms have emerged as transformative tools in the modern workplace, especially as we prepare for Generation Alpha's entrance. In an era where attention spans are shorter and the demand for flexibility has never been higher, microlearning and online platforms offer a uniquely effective approach to continuous education and skills development.

Microlearning breaks down educational content into bite-sized lessons that can typically be completed in under ten minutes. This format addresses the evolving needs of Generation Alpha, who have grown up in a fast-paced, digital environment inundated with information. Rather than traditional hour-long training sessions, imagine lessons delivered via notifications or quick, interactive videos that can be consumed between tasks.

But why is this shift significant? Generation Alpha has been raised on apps, streaming services, and social media platforms. They're used to receiving information in short bursts and have developed an uncanny ability to absorb it quickly. Microlearning taps into this behaviour, making it easier for employees to engage with and retain new material. Companies that adapt to this style of content delivery will find their training programmes far more effective and engaging.

Online platforms have amplified the effectiveness of micro-learning, providing the infrastructure for delivering and tracking educational content. Services like Learning Management Systems (LMS) and mobile learning apps allow employees to access training materials anytime, anywhere. This flexibility is crucial as remote work and hybrid models become the norm, especially for a generation comfortable with digital interfaces.

The versatility of online platforms doesn't just stop at accessibility. These platforms often include interactive elements such as quizzes, discussion boards, and gamified learning experiences. Such features can enhance engagement and facilitate a deeper understanding of the material. For Gen Alpha, who are familiar with gamification in their leisure activities, this approach can make learning feel less like a chore and more like an enjoyable challenge.

Consider, for example, a scenario where your team needs to learn a new software tool. A microlearning approach might involve short tutorials, each focusing on a specific feature of the software. These could be supplemented by interactive quizzes to reinforce understanding and forums for discussing best practices. The LMS could then track progress and provide analytics to pinpoint areas where additional training is needed.

This method isn't just about convenience; it's about efficiency. Shorter, more focused training sessions mean less downtime and a quicker return to productivity. This is particularly beneficial in a dynamic work environment where employees must frequently shift tasks. Microlearning ensures that education fits seamlessly into their workflow rather than disrupting it.

Moreover, online platforms can provide a customisable learning experience, tailored to individual needs and learning styles. Adaptive learning technologies use algorithms to adjust content based on user performance, ensuring that each employee gets the most relevant and helpful material. This personalised approach aligns perfectly with Generation Alpha's expectations of bespoke experiences in all aspects of life, from social media feeds to online shopping.

Another compelling aspect is the facilitation of collaborative learning. Online platforms enable peer-to-peer interactions and foster a culture of knowledge sharing. Generation Alpha values community and collaboration, often turning to social networks for crowdsourced advice and shared experiences. Translating this into the workplace, online platforms can host discussion forums and group projects, providing a space for employees to learn from each other.

Microlearning and online platforms are not just about training; they are critical tools for career development and lifelong learning. Generation Alpha seeks continuous growth and will gravitate towards employers who provide opportunities to acquire new skills and advance their careers. Offering a robust, dynamic training programme can be a significant draw for attracting and retaining top talent from this new generation.

The integration of microlearning and online platforms also signals to employees that their employer is forward-thinking and invested in their development. This can enhance job satisfaction and foster a sense of loyalty and commitment. When employees see that their learning needs are being met in an innovative and accessible way, they're more likely to feel valued and engaged in their work.

Importantly, these platforms can also support a broader curriculum that goes beyond technical skills to include soft skills like communication, creativity, and critical thinking. Generation Alpha is likely to face a future where these soft skills are highly prized. Interactive online courses and microlearning modules can effectively teach these competencies, making employees more adaptable and versatile in their roles.

The role of employers in supporting continuous education cannot be overstated. By adopting microlearning and leveraging online platforms, companies can create a culture that prioritises development and innovation. This not only prepares employees for the challenges of today but also equips them with the tools to navigate the uncertainties of the future. For Generation Alpha, this kind of environment is not just appealing—it's expected.

In conclusion, the combination of microlearning and online platforms represents a paradigm shift in how we approach employee education and development. As Generation Alpha steps into the workforce, these tools will be indispensable in creating an adaptable, skilled, and engaged team. Companies that embrace these innovations will find themselves not just keeping pace with change but setting the standard for the future of work.

The Role of Employers in Continuous Education is not just a checkbox item in today's corporate strategies; it's a necessity. As workplaces evolve to integrate Generation Alpha, the impetus grows stronger for employers to develop robust continuous education frameworks. Generation Alpha, shaped profoundly by rapid technological advancements and a dynamic socio-economic landscape, expects their professional environment to be as fluid and adaptive as they are. Employers have a unique responsibility to harness this expectation and turn it into a strategic advantage.

First, let's talk about *relevance*. Continuous education programs ensure that employees' skills stay up-to-date, bridging any gaps in competencies that emerge as industries evolve. When firms invest in learning initiatives, they're not just improving skill sets; they're enhancing their adaptability quotient. This translates into a more agile workforce capable of pivoting effortlessly in response to market shifts or technological disruptions.

Why is this especially critical for integrating Generation Alpha? This cohort, with their intrinsic familiarity with technology, will bring fresh perspectives and innovation to the table. Employers can tailor continuous education programs to reinforce and expand on this knowledge, promoting an environment where learning is both ubiquitous and engaging. Through well-designed learning pathways, employers can cultivate and tap into the unique potential of Generation Alpha.

Moreover, there's a profound connection between learning and employee engagement. For Generation Alpha, work isn't just about a paycheck; it's about growth, purpose, and impact. When employers prioritise continuous education, they signal a commitment to their employees' personal and professional development. This gesture fosters loyalty and can significantly reduce turnover, as employees feel valued and see a clear trajectory for their future within the organisation.

Employers also stand to gain a competitive edge by aligning their continuous education efforts with industry trends. Take the realms of AI, blockchain, or sustainable practices, for instance. These are not just buzzwords but key drivers shaping industries. By integrating such topics into learning curricula, employers ensure their workforce remains ahead of the curve, ready to tackle emerging challenges with confidence and innovation.

Let's consider the logistics. Implementing continuous education is not a one-size-fits-all approach. Employers must leverage a mix of traditional and modern learning methodologies. Online platforms, microlearning modules, and virtual reality trainings are just a few tools in the arsenal. Adaptability is key here – Generation Alpha will appreciate and thrive in environments where learning is adaptable, accessible, and aligned with cutting-edge technology.

It's also important to foster an organisational culture that champions *lifelong learning*. Employers must lead by example, demonstrating through their policies and leadership styles that learning never stops. From executive seminars to cross-functional workshops, the ethos of continuous education should permeate every layer of the organisation.

Additionally, employers can create mentorship programmes where seasoned employees guide Generation Alpha. This intergenerational exchange of skills and knowledge can be incredibly enriching. Mentors provide the wisdom and experience, while the younger generation offers fresh, tech-savvy insights. This creates a symbiotic learning environment beneficial to all parties involved.

There's also a strategic aspect to consider. Continuous education isn't just about enhancing current skills but also about anticipating future needs. Employers must engage in proactive workforce planning, identifying potential skill gaps and addressing them before they become critical. Analytical tools and market research can offer invaluable insights, helping employers craft forward-looking education initiatives.

Moreover, collaboration with educational institutions and professional bodies can offer formal recognition and certification for continuous learning efforts. These partnerships can lend credibility to in-house training programmes and provide employees with tangible proof of their competencies, further boosting morale and motivation.

But it's not just the hard skills that need attention. Soft skills, such as communication, creativity, and critical thinking, are equally crucial. Employers must ensure their education programmes encompass these areas, creating a well-rounded, versatile workforce. Generation Alpha, in particular, will benefit from such holistic development, as they navigate complex, multifaceted career landscapes.

There's also the matter of inclusivity. Tailoring continuous education programmes to meet diverse needs promotes an inclusive workplace culture. Employers should offer customised learning paths to accommodate different learning styles and career aspirations, ensuring every employee has the opportunity to thrive.

Investment in continuous education also reflects a commitment to sustainability. As businesses strive to address environmental concerns, educating employees on sustainable practices and green technologies becomes paramount. This knowledge can drive internal initiatives and foster a culture of environmental responsibility, aligning business practices with broader societal values.

And let's not forget the bottom line. Investing in continuous education can drive productivity and innovation, leading to tangible financial benefits. Employees equipped with the latest knowledge and skills are better positioned to contribute to efficiency improvements, innovative solutions, and competitive advantages.

In conclusion, the role of employers in continuous education is multifaceted and critical. It's about creating a culture of learning that not only meets the expectations of Generation Alpha but also leverages their unique strengths. By prioritising continuous education, employers can cultivate an agile, engaged, and forward-thinking workforce ready to thrive in an ever-evolving world. This investment doesn't just benefit individual employees—it paves the way for organisational success, resilience, and innovation.

Chapter 6:
The Gig Economy and Freelancing

The surge in the gig economy and freelancing isn't just a fleeting trend; it's an enduring shift that's redefining how we perceive work. Generation Alpha, with their intrinsic digital fluency and appetite for autonomy, will play a pivotal role in accelerating this movement. Imagine a workforce where the lines between traditional employment and freelancing blur, creating a dynamic ecosystem that thrives on flexibility and innovation. This shift offers unparalleled freedom for workers to dictate their own schedules and pursue various interests, yet it also poses challenges for organisational structures that have long relied on stable, full-time employment models. Employers must adapt quickly, establishing supportive frameworks to ensure gig workers receive legal rights and social protections and fostering collaborative communities through digital platforms. By embracing these changes, organisations can tap into a vast talent pool that's always ready for the next big project, driving growth, creativity, and sustainability in the workplace.

Flexibility and Freedom: The Appeal of the Gig Economy

There's something undeniably enticing about the gig economy that resonates deeply with the ethos of Generation Alpha. It's a paradigm built on flexibility and freedom, offering individuals the autonomy to craft their own careers away from traditional 9-to-5 constraints. For forward-thinking leaders, this shift presents both opportunities and challenges. The gig economy doesn't just cater to a desire for better work-life balance; it opens up a landscape where talent can be sourced globally, breaking geographical barriers. However, it's crucial to establish robust frameworks that support freelancers without sacrificing the stability and benefits typically afforded to full-time employees. By leveraging the gig economy and its inherent flexibility, companies can stay agile, innovate continuously, and attract the best of the next generation's talent while fostering a culture that values and sustains work freedom.

The Impact on Traditional Employment Models will play a pivotal role in the transformation of the workplace as Generation Alpha steps into their professional lives. As the youngest cohort to enter the workforce, their expectations and adeptness with technology will challenge longstanding employment structures. Companies will need to rethink how they attract, engage, and retain this dynamic group.

One immediate implication is the shift towards flexible work arrangements. Generation Alpha, being digital natives, expects an environment that supports remote work, flexibility, and seamless integration of life and work. The traditional 9-to-5, five-day workweek model is poised for a significant makeover. We already see a move towards hybrid work models, and this trend will only accelerate.

The gig economy will also become more prominent. For Generation Alpha, the allure of short-term, project-based work offers the possibility for growth and learning without the constraints of a permanent position. Employers will need to adapt by offering more freelance positions or risk losing out on valuable talent who prefer not to be tied down by traditional employment contracts.

Education and continuous learning will become even more central as the pace of technological advancement quickens. Generation Alpha values skills and experiences over the tenure of their predecessors. Companies must invest in training and development programs that are adaptable and ever-evolving.

The leadership paradigm will also see a shift. This new generation expects emotionally intelligent leaders who embrace inclusivity and promote a culture of constant innovation. The autocratic, top-down leadership model will likely be rejected in favour of a more collaborative and empathetic approach.

Standard performance metrics will undergo transformation. Rather than focusing solely on hours worked or the longevity of employment, success will be measured by the quality and impact of work. This shift requires rethinking incentive structures to reward creativity, problem-solving, and adaptability.

With a focus on sustainability and social responsibility, Generation Alpha's influence will bring ethical considerations to the forefront. Companies will increasingly be evaluated not just on their economic performance, but on their environmental and social impact. This shift will impact hiring processes, investment strategies, and overall corporate governance.

Traditional hiring processes will need to adapt as well. Innovative recruitment strategies incorporating advanced technologies like AI and machine learning can provide a personalised candidate experience. Moreover, the values and beliefs of Generation Alpha must be highlighted to attract the right talent.

Diversity, Equity, and Inclusion (DEI) will be non-negotiable. This generation is coming of age in a world where social justice issues are paramount. As a result, businesses will be compelled to make meaningful and tangible commitments to DEI initiatives or face backlash from the workforce and customers alike.

Yet, the transformation isn't without its challenges. Compliance with labour laws, tax regulations, and benefits administration for a more fluid workforce requires new strategic frameworks. Companies must develop systems to support gig workers and freelancers adequately.

Organisational culture will need to evolve. Hierarchical structures based on seniority and years of service may give way to network-based models that reward agility, collaboration, and innovation. Generational diversity will enrich company culture, offering diverse perspectives and ideas.

Expectations around employee well-being will change, too. Generation Alpha not only values mental and physical health but demands workplaces that prioritise them. Companies will need to adopt policies facilitating work-life balance and mental health support.

Transparency becomes an essential attribute. With access to information like never before, this generation demands transparency around corporate practices, from decision-making processes to financial health and environmental policies. Companies will be compelled to be more open with their employees.

Lastly, agile methodologies will burgeon. As the norm of employment becomes more transient, businesses will need to be nimble in adapting to frequent changes, whether technological advancements or shifting talent landscapes. Embracing agility will be crucial for staying competitive.

In essence, the integration of Generation Alpha into the workplace necessitates a holistic rethinking of traditional employment models. Forward-thinking leaders and HR professionals who recognise and adapt to these changes will find themselves at the vanguard of a new era of work, one marked by flexibility, inclusivity, and a relentless drive for innovation.

Challenges and Opportunities for Workers and Employers in the gig economy and freelancing space significantly differ from traditional employment models. As Generation Alpha emerges, both groups face unique challenges and opportunities that need addressing. These new dynamics require forward-thinking leaders to adapt with empathy and strategic foresight.

Firstly, the most obvious trend is the shift towards greater flexibility. Gen Alpha will likely favour flexible, project-based work over rigid nine-to-five schedules. While this provides opportunities for employers to tap into a diverse talent pool on-demand, it also necessitates robust project management and clear communication strategies. This generation's comfort with technology can be leveraged, but it requires consistent alignment of digital tools and human touchpoints.

Here's where it gets challenging: integrating freelancers into existing teams seamlessly. Often, full-time employees and freelancers may struggle to collaborate effectively due to differing engagement levels and work styles. Employers need to cultivate an inclusive team environment where all contributors, regardless of employment status, feel valued and aligned with the company's mission and objectives.

At the heart of effective integration lies strong communication. Employers must invest in platforms that enable transparent, real-time dialogue. Collaboration tools should support not just task management but foster informal interactions that build team cohesion. Encouraging regular virtual meetups and introducing cross-functional projects can bridge the gap between remote freelancers and onsite employees.

For workers, opportunities abound in the gig economy. Freelancers have the freedom to pick projects that align with their skills and passions, paving the way for more fulfilling career paths. However, this freedom comes with the need for self-discipline and effective time management to mitigate risks of overwork and burnout. Balancing multiple clients and projects necessitates strong organisational skills and the ability to set healthy boundaries.

Financial stability is another significant challenge. Unlike traditional employees, freelancers often do not have access to consistent income or employer-sponsored benefits. It's imperative for them to build financial resilience, perhaps through savings, insurance, or diversifying income streams. Employers can play a supportive role by offering access to financial planning resources and support services.

The gig economy also opens up opportunities for skill diversification. Unlike static roles within traditional employment, freelancing allows individuals to explore various industries and functions. This can make workers more adaptable and innovative, traits that are invaluable in today's fast-changing job market. Employers benefit by tapping into this diverse skill set, creating a more dynamic and versatile workforce.

Regulatory compliance is a growing challenge as the gig economy evolves. Employers must stay abreast of changing laws around contractors versus employees to avoid legal pitfalls. This requires a proactive approach, regularly consulting with legal experts and adapting contract templates to meet compliance standards. Freelancers, on the other hand, need to be aware of their rights and obligations, ensuring they are treated fairly and equitably.

Beyond regulation, the gig economy's rise brings ethical considerations to the fore. Employers need to cultivate equitable treatment practices to prevent exploitation of gig workers. Offering fair pay, reasonable deadlines, and transparent communication builds trust and fosters long-term relationships. Freelancers, too, should adopt ethical practices, delivering high-quality work consistently and establishing trust with their clients.

Training and development present another dual challenge and opportunity. Employers should not overlook freelancers in their training initiatives. Providing access to educational resources and upskilling opportunities can enhance overall performance and foster loyalty. For freelancers, ongoing learning is non-negotiable. Keeping abreast with industry trends and continuously upskilling ensures they remain competitive and relevant.

Work-life balance is a perennial challenge, especially in a gig economy that operates without traditional boundaries. Freelancers often find themselves working round-the-clock to meet diverse client demands. Employers can help by setting clear expectations and respecting freelancers' personal time. Creating a culture that values work-life harmony supports the well-being of both freelancers and full-time employees.

The opportunity to innovate is a hallmark advantage in the gig economy. Both freelancers and employers can benefit from adopting agile methodologies that support rapid innovation cycles. Freelancers can bring fresh perspectives and novel solutions, while employers can provide creative briefs and problem statements that challenge conventional thinking. This symbiotic relationship encourages continual learning and adaptation.

Addressing psychological safety is also crucial. Freelancers often work in isolation, which can lead to feelings of detachment and reduced motivation. Employers must foster an inclusive culture where everyone, including gig workers, feels psychologically safe to share ideas, ask questions, and admit mistakes without fear of retribution. This involves training leaders to be empathetic and creating feedback mechanisms that genuinely consider freelancers' inputs.

Technology will be a game-changer in the freelancer-employer dynamic. Employers need to invest in advanced digital platforms that facilitate effective collaboration and communication. Such tools should not only manage tasks but also provide analytics to monitor engagement, productivity, and satisfaction levels. For workers, fluency in multiple collaborative tools can be a significant advantage, making them more versatile and attractive to diverse clients.

Lastly, the gig economy encourages a results-oriented mindset. Employers can benefit from focusing on outcomes rather than processes, which is often more critical in project-based work. This approach also aligns well with the gig worker's objective to deliver high-quality results within stipulated timelines. Emphasising outcomes over rigid procedural adherence fosters a more innovative and productive work environment.

In summary, the rise of the gig economy brings a multitude of challenges and opportunities for both workers and employers. Navigating this landscape requires adaptability, strong communication, and a commitment to continuous learning. Employers and freelancers who embrace these principles will not only thrive but also foster a collaborative ecosystem that drives innovation and success in the future workplace.

Building a Supportive Framework for Freelancers

To truly embrace the potential of the gig economy and freelancing within your organisation, building a supportive framework is imperative. Employers need to construct an environment that not only accommodates but also champions these non-traditional workers. This involves providing legal rights and social protections akin to those enjoyed by full-time employees, creating a level playing field. Establishing platforms and communities where freelancers can connect, share knowledge, and collaborate will cultivate a sense of belonging and solidarity. By doing so, companies not only attract top-tier freelance talent but also foster a culture of innovation and adaptability. The end goal is a workplace landscape where flexibility isn't just a perk but a standard—one that embraces sustainability and the dynamic contributions of Generation Alpha, reshaping the future of work in profound and lasting ways.

Legal Rights and Social Protection are paramount in any discussion about the future of work. With the rise of the gig economy and freelance work, it's essential to address the unique legal and social challenges that Generation Alpha will face. As forward-thinking leaders, you need to prepare a work environment where these young professionals can thrive, knowing their rights are safeguarded and social protections are robust.

Firstly, the burgeoning gig economy brings an array of opportunities but also some significant concerns. The flexibility and freedom it provides are attractive, but these come at the cost of traditional employment benefits. Gen Alpha workers will need clear legal frameworks to protect their interests.

Existing labour laws are often not equipped to deal with the nuances of gig work, necessitating updates and new legislation.

One of the critical issues here is the lack of social security benefits for freelancers. Traditional employees enjoy rights to healthcare, retirement savings, and unemployment benefits, which are often not extended to gig workers. As HR professionals, the onus will be on you to advocate for and potentially help design new policies that ensure Gen Alpha freelancers are not left vulnerable.

Moreover, the classification of gig workers itself is a contentious issue. Should they be considered employees or independent contractors? This distinction affects everything from tax obligations to eligibility for benefits. Advances in legal definitions and protections are crucial for providing clear and fair guidelines, reducing the risk of exploitation in the gig economy.

Another significant area is the implementation of standardised contracts. Many gig workers deal with opaque agreements that can lead to unfair working conditions. Transparent, standardised contracts that clearly outline workers' rights and responsibilities will be critical in this new work landscape. Contract transparency can provide a layer of protection, making sure everyone is on the same page.

Additionally, dispute resolution mechanisms need to be in place. Traditional employment structures offer processes for addressing grievances, which are largely absent in gig work. Establishing reliable and accessible dispute resolution services will be essential. These can range from mediation practices to legal avenues, ensuring that gig workers have recourse when needed.

Social protection is not just about legal rights; it's about creating supportive networks. Community hubs, either physical or virtual, can offer gig workers spaces to collaborate, learn, and support each other. Such platforms can be invaluable resources for Gen Alpha, fostering a sense of community and shared purpose.

Next, let's consider health and safety regulations. Unlike traditional workplaces, gig workers often operate independently, making the enforcement of safety standards tricky. Developing industry-specific guidelines and implementing regular safety checks can go a long way in ensuring the well-being of these workers. This is particularly important for jobs involving physical labour or driving, where risks are higher.

One cannot overlook the role of technology in providing social protection. Platforms that facilitate gig work should also be responsible for ensuring worker protections. They can offer insurance options, track working hours to prevent burnout, and use algorithms to flag potentially exploitative practices. Transparency in how these platforms operate is crucial; they should be required to disclose how their algorithms impact work allocation and compensation.

Moreover, educational resources are a vital part of social protection. Gig workers should have access to training that helps them understand their rights and responsibilities. Platforms can offer modules on financial planning, legal rights, and even health and safety. These educational resources can empower workers to make informed decisions, thereby enhancing their long-term stability.

Diversification of income sources also needs to be encouraged. Relying on a single gig platform can be risky; diversification can mitigate some of these risks. Encouraging workers to engage with multiple platforms and providing them with tools to manage this can enhance their financial security.

Financial literacy programmes can further aid in this diversification effort, teaching workers to save and invest wisely.

Next, there's the issue of mental health. Gig economy work can often be isolating, leading to stress and mental health issues. Offering mental health support, either through online counselling services or peer support groups, can make a significant difference. Mental health should be seen as integral to social protection, not as an optional extra.

The role of government and regulatory bodies cannot be overstated. It is imperative for them to collaborate with businesses and worker representatives to create a fair and inclusive environment. Policymakers need to be agile, updating regulations in real-time to keep pace with the fast-evolving world of gig work.

In summary, **Legal Rights and Social Protection** for Generation Alpha in the gig economy aren't just a nice-to-have; they are fundamental to creating a fair and sustainable future of work. From updating legal frameworks to providing mental and financial support structures, the path forward involves multiple stakeholders coming together. As leaders and strategists, your role in advocating for these protections is crucial, ensuring that Generation Alpha doesn't just survive but thrives in the new world of work.

Platforms and Communities for Collaboration have reshaped how we think about work and teamwork, especially in the context of the gig economy. As we navigate through the transition toward more flexible employment models, understanding these platforms and communities becomes not just optional but essential. With Generation Alpha set to enter the workforce, there's a growing need for workplaces that are as adaptable, innovative, and inclusive as the individuals joining them. This section aims to provide insights into how collabor-ation platforms and online communities can bridge these gaps and create a robust support system for gig workers.

First, let's talk about the nature of collaboration platforms themselves. Tools like Slack, Trello, and Microsoft Teams have become ubiquitous in modern workspaces, offering streamlined communication and project management capabilities. However, their potential to create an inclusive and collaborative environment for gig workers is still being fully realized. These platforms enable seamless interaction among team members regardless of their location, facilitating real-time collaboration on projects. This virtual integration is crucial in a gig economy where flexibility and remote interaction are often prioritised over traditional office setups.

Unlike earlier generations, Generation Alpha is growing up with an inherent familiarity with technology. This demographic's adeptness with digital tools makes platforms that offer file sharing, video conferencing, and instant messaging essential rather than supplementary. For HR professionals and team leaders, selecting the right platform becomes a strategic decision. It's not just about facilitating day-to-day operations but also about ensuring ongoing engagement and collaboration among a workforce that's increasingly distributed and diverse.

A critical aspect of these platforms is their ability to create a sense of community among gig workers. The importance of community can't be overstated, especially for freelancers who might otherwise feel isolated. Online communities like those found on LinkedIn, Reddit, or industry-specific forums provide spaces for freelancers to share expertise, seek advice, and even find new opportunities. These communities foster peer support systems that can mitigate the uncertainties and challenges that come with freelance work.

Online communities can also serve as incubators for innovation and professional development. They offer avenues for talent to collaborate on projects, share insights, and stay updated on industry trends. For Generation Alpha, continually evolving in their roles and skills through such forums will be second nature. These platforms can become vital sources of continuous learning, networking, and professional growth, helping young workers navigate a fluid and unpredictable job market.

Another important factor is how these platforms and communities can promote sustainability and social responsibility. Many collaboration platforms now incorporate features that encourage eco-friendly practices, such as digital documentation, virtual meetings, and project tracking. This aligns well with Generation Alpha's values around sustainability and environmental responsibility. By leveraging these tools, companies can reduce their carbon footprint and demonstrate their commitment to responsible practices, which is likely to resonate deeply with young gig workers.

Building trust and providing a sense of job security are paramount in the gig economy. With the right collaborative platforms, employers can offer transparency regarding project scopes, timelines, and payment processes. Blockchain technology, for instance, can be employed for transparent and secure transactions, building trust amongst freelancers. These measures not only instill confidence but also foster long-term working relationships that can be more fruitful for both the gig worker and the employer.

Moreover, collaboration platforms can aid in mentoring and peer learning. Generation Alpha workers will benefit from structures that allow for mentorship in a remote setup. Through video calls, shared documents, and collaborative tasks, senior team members can guide less experienced freelancers, helping them develop their skills and grow within their roles. Platforms that support such interactions will be key in nurturing the next generation of talent, ensuring they feel valued and connected despite the physical distances.

The psychological well-being of gig workers is another area where collaboration platforms and communities can make a significant impact. Isolation and a lack of peer interaction are common challenges faced by freelancers. Integrating social features such as virtual water coolers, chat rooms, and team-building activities in these platforms can help break the monotony and foster a sense of belonging. These digital social spaces can replicate the camaraderie of traditional office environments, making gig workers feel less isolated and more integrated into the team.

Furthermore, platforms and communities that focus on inclusivity and diversity can attract a broader talent pool. Generation Alpha values diversity and inclusion, and they expect their workplaces to reflect these values. Platforms that feature inclusive practices, equitable processes, and diverse representation can help companies attract and retain top young talent. Moderated forums and grievance redressal features within these communities can ensure that all voices are heard and respected, further enhancing the collaborative ecosystem.

In the pursuit of fostering seamless collaboration, employers should also consider integrating AI-driven analytics with their chosen platforms. AI can help in tracking work patterns, identifying bottlenecks, and even predicting future project needs. For Generation

Alpha, who are accustomed to the presence of AI in their daily lives, these intelligent features can enhance productivity and reduce inefficiencies. By offering actionable insights, AI can enable more informed decision-making and streamline collaborative efforts.

Looking at the bigger picture, these platforms can facilitate global collaboration, breaking down geographical barriers. As businesses become more global, having a diverse team that collaborates effectively across time zones becomes a strategic advantage. With tools that offer real-time collaboration and asynchronous communication options, gig workers from different parts of the world can work together seamlessly. This not only broadens the talent pool but also brings in diverse perspectives that can drive innovation.

Employers need to remain agile in adapting these platforms to serve the evolving needs of their workforce. Continuous feedback loops, where gig workers can voice their needs and concerns about the platforms, can drive improvements and ensure that these tools remain relevant and effective. Flexibility in adopting and integrating new technologies as they emerge will also be crucial in staying ahead of the curve and maintaining a competitive edge.

Lastly, fostering collaboration extends beyond just platforms and tools; it involves cultivating a culture of mutual respect, open communication, and shared goals. Leaders should emphasise the importance of collaboration in their organisational culture, encouraging gig workers to engage and contribute actively. Recognising and rewarding collaborative efforts can further motivate freelancers and instil a sense of belonging and accomplishment.

In closing, **Platforms and Communities for Collaboration** are not just about technology; they're about creating an environment where every worker, gig or otherwise, feels valued and included. As we move towards a future where Generation Alpha integrates into our workplace, harnessing the potential of these platforms will be crucial in fostering innovation, flexibility, and long-term success. By staying informed and adaptable, leaders can build work environments that not only meet the needs of the present but are also resilient for the future.

Chapter 7:
Diversity, Equity, and Inclusion (DEI)

Generation Alpha, poised to enter the workforce, will bring with them an insistent demand for diversity, equity, and inclusion, changing the very DNA of corporate culture. To truly integrate these young talents, organisations need to go beyond tokenism, embedding genuine DEI strategies that celebrate varied perspectives and promote fairness at every level. It's not just about ticking boxes; it's about creating environments where everyone feels valued and heard. By addressing unconscious biases and fostering equitable practices, firms can unlock the innovative potential that diverse teams naturally offer. When DEI is prioritised, it's not merely a moral imperative—it's a strategic advantage. Companies that embrace this will find themselves better positioned to navigate global markets, draw from a broader talent pool, and drive sustained growth and innovation. The journey won't be easy, it requires a commitment to continuous education, open dialogue, and the courage to challenge the status quo, but the rewards will echo across generations, setting a precedent for a more inclusive and dynamic future workplace.

Beyond Tokenism: Genuine Inclusion Strategies

To move beyond tokenism and create genuinely inclusive workplaces, organisations must adopt strategies that transcend mere diversity metrics. It's about fostering an environment where every individual feels valued and empowered to contribute fully, irrespective of their background. This involves taking a hard look at existing practices and consciously addressing unconscious biases. Mentorship programmes, diverse hiring panels, and employee-resource groups can play a pivotal role in bridging gaps. Furthermore, education on cultural competencies and equitable policies must be ingrained into the company's ethos. By implementing these strategies, companies will not just fulfil ethical obligations but will also unleash a wave of innovation and engagement that drives long-term growth and success. Through deliberate and mindful efforts, genuine inclusion transforms from a box-ticking exercise to a substantive, organisation-wide commitment, ultimately fostering a workplace where everyone can thrive.

Creating Inclusive Workplaces for Diverse Talent is more than a mandate; it's a strategy for sustainability and growth. As we welcome Generation Alpha—a group defined by its digital fluency, diversity, and socially conscious mindset—into the workforce, creating inclusive environments becomes not just essential but transformative. This generation's expectation for inclusivity will reshape organisational cultures, resulting in workplaces where every individual feels valued and empowered to contribute.

To build these inclusive workplaces, leaders and HR professionals must start by understanding what inclusivity means for Generation Alpha. This is a generation that doesn't just tolerate diversity—they celebrate it. They've grown up in a world where conversations about gender identity, racial equity, and accessibility are not just commonplace but critical. Therefore, organisations must move beyond mere tokenism and implement genuine, systemic changes that foster inclusion at every level.

Firstly, hiring practices must evolve. Companies need to adopt blind recruitment processes where personal identifiers are hidden during initial screening stages. This practice helps mitigate unconscious biases that often permeate hiring decisions. Diversity should not stop at recruitment; it should be reflected in retention and promotion policies. Offering mentorship programmes, career development workshops, and leadership training specifically aimed at underepresented groups can make a significant impact.

Next, create spaces for open dialogue. Establishing employee resource groups (ERGs) can provide a platform for marginalised voices and ensure they are heard at the highest levels of decision-making. These groups can act as task forces to identify gaps in inclusivity efforts and propose actionable solutions. Encourage your employees to share their cultural experiences and perspectives through storytelling sessions or cross-cultural workshops, promoting mutual understanding and appreciation.

Transparency is another cornerstone of inclusivity. Use data to create accountability. Regularly publish diversity and inclusion metrics, showing where your company stands and the progress you are making. This data should be accessible to all employees, fostering a culture of transparency and continual improvement. Metrics can include the diversity of new hires, employee retention rates across different demographics, and employee satisfaction scores regarding inclusivity.

Diverse talent also requires flexible work policies. Generation Alpha prioritises work-life balance and values employers who offer flexibility. Remote work options, flexible hours, and a results-oriented approach instead of a rigid 9-to-5 schedule can make your organisation more attractive to a diverse workforce. Importantly, ensure that such policies are equitable and accessible to all employees, regardless of their role or seniority.

And let's not forget technology. Inclusivity in the digital age means ensuring all employees have equal access to the tools and resources they need to succeed. This includes IT support for remote workers, ergonomic equipment for home offices, and accessibility tools for employees with disabilities. Invest in platforms that support various communication styles, from text-based messaging to video calls, to cater to the diverse needs of your team.

Fostering psychological safety is essential. Employees should feel safe to express their ideas, take risks, and fail without fear of ostracism. Create an environment where feedback is not just welcomed but encouraged—and implement it constructively. Regular check-ins, anonymous surveys, and an open-door policy can go a long way in making employees feel heard and valued.

Leadership plays a crucial role in championing inclusivity. Leaders must set the tone by embodying inclusive behaviours themselves. Training programmes focused on emotional intelligence, cultural competence, and bias awareness are crucial for leaders to effectively manage diverse teams. A leader who acknowledges their own biases and actively works to overcome them can inspire their team to do the same.

Moreover, inclusive workplaces benefit immensely from diversity of thought, driving innovation and problem-solving. When you bring together individuals from different backgrounds, perspectives, and skillsets, you create fertile ground for creative solutions that a homogenous group might not conceive. This diversity of thought can give your company a competitive edge, driving growth and adaptation in an ever-changing market.

Commitment to inclusivity should also extend into company policies and corporate social responsibility (CSR) initiatives. Employees need to see that their values align with organisational actions. This could mean supporting community initiatives, advocating for social justice causes, or implementing environmentally sustainable practices. Such actions not only fortify employee engagement but also attract Generation Alpha talent whose values resonate with these missions.

Moreover, don't overlook the importance of inclusive language. Language shapes culture, and inclusive language ensures everyone feels respected and valued. Train employees to use gender-neutral terms and avoid language that could inadvertently marginalise any group. Simple changes in communication can have profound effects on workplace culture.

Finally, remember that inclusivity is an ongoing journey, not a tick-box exercise. Continuous improvement should be at the core of your strategy. Regularly revisit and update your inclusivity policies, considering the evolving needs and values of your diverse workforce. Solicit feedback, measure impact, and be prepared to pivot your approach as necessary.

In summary, creating an inclusive workplace for diverse talent is both an ethical responsibility and a strategic advantage. As Generation Alpha enters the workforce, their expectations will elevate standards of diversity and inclusion across industries. By fostering a culture where everyone feels valued and empowered, organisations won't just adapt—they'll thrive. The future of work is diverse, inclusive, and equitable, setting the stage for unprecedented innovation and collaboration.

Addressing Unconscious Bias and Promoting Equity is pivotal for creating workplaces where Generation Alpha can truly thrive and contribute. This new generation, with its innate awareness and advocacy for inclusivity, will expect workplaces to not just pay lip service to equity, but to embed it into the very fabric of organisational culture.

Unconscious bias, those implicit attitudes or stereotypes that affect our understanding, actions, and decisions, is not a new challenge. However, addressing it in modern workplaces has never been more critical. For Generation Alpha, equality and fairness are non-negotiables. They have grown up in an era where diversity is celebrated, and they expect their professional environments to reflect these values.

Promoting equity means being proactive rather than reactive. Instead of waiting for problems to surface, organisations should be conducting regular bias training and audits. These should extend beyond tick-box exercises and seek real, actionable insights. By doing so, organisations can create transparent systems that recognise and reward talent fairly. Leaders and HR professionals must leverage data analytics tools to identify patterns of bias that might not be apparent at first glance.

Emphasising diverse hiring practices is just the beginning. Once diverse talent is onboarded, it's crucial to ensure they are given equal opportunities to advance. Unfortunately, many organisations falter by failing to provide legitimate pathways for growth. Mentorship programmmes, diversity councils, and sponsorship initiatives are practical tools to cultivate a supportive environment for all employees, especially those from underrepresented groups.

Building an equitable workplace isn't solely a top-down approach. Encouraging employees at all levels to participate in conversations about bias and equity fosters a collective responsibility. This can be facilitated through inclusive forums, where employees feel safe to voice their concerns and share their experiences. It's about creating a culture where equity is everyone's business.

The role of leadership cannot be understated. Leaders must model the behaviour they wish to see. For Generation Alpha, seeing leaders who actively champion diversity and fairness sets a powerful precedent. Transparent communication from leaders about the steps being taken to address unconscious bias builds trust and demonstrates a commitment to meaningful change.

Organisations must also be mindful of the evolving nature of bias. With changing social dynamics, new biases can emerge. Continuous education and awareness training help ensure that everyone, from C-suite executives to entry-level employees, remains aware and sensitive to these shifts. Bias training that incorporates real-world scenarios and ongoing learning modules is more effective than one-off sessions.

Utilising technology can also play a significant role in mitigating unconscious bias. AI and machine learning tools can assist in creating more objective hiring processes, performance evaluations, and promotion pathways. By reducing human subjectivity in these crucial areas, organisations can move closer to achieving genuine equity.

Moreover, it's essential to measure and track progress. Organisations should establish clear metrics to evaluate the effectiveness of their equity initiatives. Regular reporting and openness about these metrics can drive accountability and continuous improvement. Leaders should be prepared to adapt strategies based on these evaluations and feedback from their workforce.

Creating equitable workplaces also calls for an intersectional approach to diversity. It's not enough to consider only one dimension of diversity, such as gender or race, in isolation. Understanding how various identities intersect can provide deeper insights into the unique challenges that different groups may face. Training and policies should reflect this nuanced understanding.

Generation Alpha will enter the workforce with expectations for genuine action, not just promises. For forward-thinking leaders and HR professionals, this is an opportunity to build a workplace environment that attracts and retains top talent. Demonstrating a genuine commitment to equity can serve as a powerful differentiator in a competitive job market.

Long-term, embedding equity into the organisational DNA can drive innovation, creativity, and performance. Diverse teams bring varied perspectives that can lead to unique solutions and break-throughs. The benefits of these diverse contributions can significantly outweigh the effort it takes to address and dismantle unconscious biases.

Finally, promoting equity and addressing unconscious bias isn't just a moral imperative – it's a strategic one. Organisations that excel in these areas will not only align with Generation Alpha's values but will also set themselves up for sustained success through an engaged, diverse, and motivated workforce.

As we transition into a future where Generation Alpha steps into their roles, let's ensure we're prepared to meet their expectations with a framework built on fairness and equality. By doing so, we set the stage for a more innovative, inclusive, and prosperous workplace for all.

In the subsequent sections, we'll delve into the various aspects of how DEI can confer competitive advantages and how global perspectives can enhance our understanding of diversity. The journey toward a truly equitable workplace is ongoing, but with the right tools and commitment, it's a goal well within our reach.

DEI as a Competitive Advantage

When it comes to embracing Generation Alpha in the workplace, leveraging Diversity, Equity, and Inclusion (DEI) can be your competitive edge. It's not just about moral imperatives; DEI fuels innovation, fosters diverse perspectives, and enhances problem-solving capabilities. Imagine a workspace where every individual, irrespective of their background, feels valued and empowered to contribute. Such environments are breeding grounds for creativity and ingenuity. When businesses are authentically inclusive, they attract top-tier talent from a broad spectrum, leading to richer ideation and robust decision-making. Moreover, organisations that prioritise DEI are better equipped to understand and cater to a globalised market, translating into enhanced customer satisfaction and loyalty. Essentially, DEI isn't just a box to tick; it's a strategic advantage that drives sustained growth and resilience in an ever-evolving corporate landscape. Let's harness the transformative power of DEI to sculpt a future that's not only inclusive but extraordinarily successful.

The Business Case for Diversity and Innovation is not just a trendy buzzword or a box-ticking exercise. It's a strategic imperative that fuels growth, drives sustainability, and enhances the bottom line. For forward-thinking leaders, HR professionals, and strategists, investing in diversity is akin to pouring high-octane fuel into the engine of innovation. Here's why it's not just beneficial but essential in ushering Generation Alpha into the workplace.

Diverse teams bring a plethora of perspectives, experiences, and skills to the table. This mix of minds creates fertile ground for fresh ideas and innovative solutions. When people from different back-grounds collaborate, they challenge the status quo, push boundaries, and find novel ways to tackle existing problems. In essence, diversity is the secret ingredient to creativity and innovation.

Incorporating Generation Alpha, a cohort that values authenticity and inclusivity, into diverse teams magnifies these benefits. This generation, characterised by their digital nativity and environmental consciousness, thrives in environments that celebrate differences and drive forward-thinking solutions. They are not mere cogs in a machine but catalysts for transformational change.

Research indicates that companies with diverse leadership are 33% more likely to see better-than-average profits. This statistic alone underscores how diversity translates to direct financial gain. It's not just about the ethical high ground; it's about smart business practice. Diverse teams understand and cater to equally diverse consumer bases more effectively, tapping into new markets and enhancing customer satisfaction.

Moreover, Generation Alpha will likely gravitate towards organisations with strong diversity and inclusion policies. They are not just looking for a pay cheque; they are looking for workplaces that mirror their values. Organisations that fail to cultivate such an environment risk falling behind in the race for top talent.

Given the pace at which technologies evolve, innovation is a continuous requirement rather than a one-off event. Diverse teams are better equipped to keep up with this rapid evolution. The various perspectives they bring can help foresee and adapt to technological advancements, ensuring the organisation remains competitive. Generation Alpha will play a crucial role in this, given their unparalleled familiarity with digital landscapes.

While the moral and ethical arguments for diversity are compelling, the business case is equally robust. Beyond enhanced creativity and profitability, diverse teams contribute to improved employee satisfaction and retention. When employees feel seen, heard, and valued, they are more likely to stay with the company, reducing turnover rates and saving on recruitment and training costs.

Innovation often entails risk, but diverse teams mitigate this by offering multiple lenses through which to view potential challenges and solutions. They are better able to anticipate issues that a more homogenous team might overlook. This breadth of vision allows for more robust, resilient strategies that stand up to stress tests, making the organisation more agile and adaptable.

Diversity is also a hedge against conformity and the pitfalls it brings. Homogenous teams might fall into groupthink, where dissenting opinions are stifled, and innovation stagnates. By contrast, diverse teams are fertile ground for constructive dissent and dialogue, crucial components of innovation. Generation Alpha, with their penchant for questioning norms, further invigorates this dynamic.

The business case for diversity is not confined to internal innovation; it extends to customer engagement as well. Teams that reflect the diversity of their customer base can deliver more relevant and compelling products and services. They can anticipate customer needs, customise offerings, and foster stronger, more authentic connections. This congruence between internal diversity and external engagement creates a virtuous cycle of innovation and customer satisfaction.

Investing in diversity and fostering an inclusive culture can also enhance an organisation's brand reputation. Companies that are seen as leaders in diversity and inclusion often enjoy a halo effect, attracting not just talent but also customers, partners, and investors. This positive brand equity further reinforces the business case for diversity, making it a cornerstone of sustainable growth.

In conclusion, **The Business Case for Diversity and Innovation** goes beyond moral obligation or regulatory compliance. It's a strategic necessity that enriches the workforce, drives innovation, and bolsters financial performance. For leaders, HR professionals, and strategists on the cusp of integrating Generation Alpha into the workplace, understanding and acting on this business case are imperative. By embracing diversity actively and authentically, organisations can unlock unprecedented potential and pave the way for a future where innovation, flexibility, and sustainability thrive.

As we welcome Generation Alpha, let's commit to harnessing the power of diversity to pave the way for groundbreaking innovation. Empowered by the rich tapestry of perspectives and experiences, these young professionals, alongside seasoned experts, will redefine the paradigms of the workplace.

The business case for diversity is clear. It's not an ancillary agenda; it's at the core of what will make the next era of work truly revolutionary. As we look forward to a future replete with challenges and opportunities, diverse and inclusive teams will be our most valuable asset. They will drive the creative solutions and sustainable practices that will keep organisations not just surviving but thriving in the ever-evolving landscape of work.

Generation Alpha is ready. The question now is, are you prepared to harness the immense potential that diversity brings? Embrace it, celebrate it, and watch as your organisation transcends limits and achieves unparalleled success in a world that increasingly values not just what you do but how and why you do it.

Now is the time to act, to build teams that reflect the world we live in, and to foster cultures where every voice is heard and valued. By doing so, we not only honour the unique contributions of each individual but also set the stage for extraordinary innovation and growth.

Diversity isn't just a business strategy. It's the key to unlocking a future where possibilities are limitless, and success is measured not just in profits but in the richness of ideas and the impact we create together. Let's make the business case for diversity not just an argument but a lived reality in every facet of the workplace.

Global Perspectives: Learning from Different Cultures enable us to unearth new ideas and approaches that could redefine the very fabric of our workplaces. As Generation Alpha steps into the professional world, their integration will demand not just an understanding of their unique characteristics and values but also a recognition of cultural diversity's tremendous potential.

Incorporating lessons from various cultural paradigms can act as a catalyst for innovation and inclusivity. When we peel back the layers of different societies, it becomes evident that distinct cultural approaches to work and collaboration can provide us with a rich tapestry of insights. For instance, the emphasis on collective well-being in many Eastern cultures could lend itself to more cohesive and supportive team dynamics. Similarly, the less formal working relationships often seen in Scandinavian countries can encourage open communication and creativity.

Imagine a corporate environment that blends the innovation-driven mentality of Silicon Valley with the meticulous project management practices found in German enterprises. The result would likely be an ecosystem where creativity thrives but structured processes ensure that imaginative ideas are effectively implemented. Such a blend could prove transformative, particularly as Generation Alpha, with their affinity for flexibility and digital fluency, finds its footing.

Consider the Japanese concept of "Kaizen," which focuses on continuous improvement through small, incremental changes. Applied globally, this approach can instil a culture of persistent development, enhancing overall productivity and efficiency. This method aligns perfectly with Generation Alpha's propensity for lifelong learning and adaptability. Kaizen isn't merely about processes and systems; it extends to people management. Imagine the immense potential unlocked when employees across the globe adopt a mindset geared towards perpetual growth.

Another cultural practice worth integrating is the African philosophy of "Ubuntu," which broadly translates to "I am because we are." It centres on the belief in a shared humanity and mutual respect, which can dramatically improve team cohesion and inclusivity. Generation Alpha is drawn to workplaces that value social responsibility. By adopting "Ubuntu," businesses can build environments where collaboration and collective success become the norms rather than the exceptions.

Additionally, the Scandinavian principle of "Janteloven," which promotes humility and discourages individual ego, can be part of building egalitarian teams. Scandinavian countries often rank among the happiest and most productive globally, and integrating elements of their work culture can lead to happier, more balanced employees. It aligns seamlessly with Generation Alpha's value of work-life balance and mental well-being, allowing them to feel both valued and productive.

Exploring these global perspectives isn't just a theoretical exercise; it's a practical necessity for modern leaders, HR professionals, and strategists. Understanding cultural nuances and intertwining them into corporate structures can bridge gaps that traditional methods might otherwise widen. As Generation Alpha enters the workplace, they will bring their global consciousness to the table. Companies globalising their organisational cultures will be better positioned to engage this new workforce effectively.

For a forward-thinking leader, integrating such global principles will require deliberate effort and genuine openness to change. Cultural training programs can be developed, wherein employees from various backgrounds share insights into their cultural mindset and working styles. Such initiatives not only foster inclusivity but also empower employees to bring their authentic selves to work, thereby increasing engagement and satisfaction.

Furthermore, embracing a multi-cultural perspective can uncover novel solutions to existing workplace challenges. For example, many companies struggle with hierarchical structures that stifle innovation and hinder communication. Implementing flatter organisational structures, a concept borrowed from tech startups in Israel, could resolve these issues. Coupled with Generation Alpha's preference for more democratic and transparent practices, this could foster a more open and innovative workplace.

The advent of digital and remote work models opens another dimension for cultural integration. When teams span continents, they bring diverse perspectives that can heighten creativity and problem-solving. However, for this diversity to be a true strength, it must be consciously managed. Tools like AI-driven language translation and cultural sensitivity training can smooth interactions and help teams harness their full potential.

Global collaboration also necessitates the reevaluation of traditional metrics of success. Instead of solely focusing on financial outcomes, companies could incorporate metrics reflecting employee engagement, innovation rates, and social impact. These metrics, derived from various cultural values, offer a more holistic picture of organisational health, resonating well with Generation Alpha's broader view of success.

An important aspect of learning from different cultures is recognising and addressing unconscious bias. For workplaces to truly be inclusive, leaders must be proactive in identifying and mitigating biases that hinder equity. This could involve implicit bias training and establishing frameworks for equitable practices. As Generation Alpha prioritises fairness and inclusion, eliminating such biases becomes crucial for attracting and retaining top talent from this cohort.

Moreover, integrating global perspectives enables businesses to build resilience. Different cultural approaches to problem-solving and crisis management can lend invaluable strategies during turbulent times. Whether it's the collective resilience seen in community-driven cultures or the structured contingency planning prevalent in countries like Switzerland, these insights can prepare workplaces to navigate uncertainties effectively.

Perhaps one of the most inspiring aspects of learning from various cultures is the opportunity it presents to create a uniquely enriched workplace. When employees feel their cultural backgrounds are not just acknowledged but celebrated, they're more likely to contribute meaningfully. This cultural celebration could manifest in many ways—from international-themed team-building events to incorporating diverse holiday celebrations into the company calendar.

In conclusion, as we prepare to welcome Generation Alpha into our workplaces, the insights gained from various cultural paradigms will be instrumental. Not only will they help in creating more inclusive and innovative environments, but they will also ensure that the workplaces of the future are places where everyone, irrespective of their background, feels valued and empowered. By learning from different cultures, leaders can build robust, dynamic, and forward-thinking organisations ready to thrive in an interconnected world.

Chapter 8:
Health and Well-being

Health and well-being are no longer peripheral concerns but central to the fabric of a thriving workplace, especially with the coming of Generation Alpha. In this new landscape, mental health isn't just a matter of nice-to-have initiatives; it's an essential organisational priority. Supporting mental resilience and providing robust strategies for a healthy work environment can significantly improve both morale and productivity. Leaders play a crucial role here, fostering a culture that prioritises well-being and destigmatises mental health challenges. Alongside this, physical health and work-life balance need the spotlight. Encouraging physical activity and investing in ergonomic solutions aren't just about preventing injury; they're about showing employees that their health matters. Flexible work schedules can also help employees juggle their responsibilities without sacrificing their well-being. By consciously integrating these elements into workplace culture, organisations can become not only more productive but also more attractive to this new generation that values holistic well-being above all else.

Mental Health at the Forefront

When it comes to reshaping the workplace for Generation Alpha, we can't afford to overlook the critical importance of mental health. This emerging generation is growing up in an era where mental well-being is considered as vital as physical health, if not more. Their openness about mental health challenges and innovative approaches to addressing them are setting new standards. Leaders and HR professionals must prioritise creating an environment where mental health is at the forefront, fostering a culture of support, understanding, and proactive intervention. It's crucial to establish robust frameworks and provide accessible resources for mental health support, ensuring employees feel safe to express vulnerabilities without judgement. Investing in mental well-being will not only enhance the overall happiness and productivity of the workforce but also cultivate a sense of loyalty and belonging among Generation Alpha, driving long-term success. Mental health shouldn't be an afterthought – it should be integrated into the very fabric of organisational culture, marking a substantial shift from traditional paradigms and paving the way for a more resilient, compassionate workplace.

Strategies for Support and Resilience are crucial in fostering a thriving work environment for Generation Alpha. As leaders and HR professionals, creating a culture where our youngest workforce feels supported and resilient is not just a nice-to-have but a necessity. Given Generation Alpha's unique characteristics, an empathic and innovative approach is paramount.

First, it's vital to understand that Generation Alpha has been raised in a digital era, where accessibility to information and social interconnectedness are at their peak. This reality shapes their expectations, including the need for mental health support. Organisations should therefore provide comprehensive mental wellness programs, including access to online therapy sessions and mental health days.

But it's not just about availability; it's about breaking the stigma. Leaders must openly discuss mental health, encouraging a culture where talking about struggles is not taboo. Through workshops, seminars, and regular check-ins, employees can feel there is a genuine concern for their wellbeing.

Moreover, mentorship programmes that pair Generation Alpha with more experienced colleagues can be incredibly beneficial. This intergenerational exchange not only helps in skills transfer but also provides emotional support and builds a sense of belonging. Simply put, when Generation Alpha feels integrated and understood, they're more likely to thrive.

On the practical side, flexible work arrangements cannot be overstated. Growing up in a world where physical and digital spaces blend seamlessly means this generation expects the same fluidity in their work environment. Offering options for remote work or hybrid models isn't just a perk; it's a necessity. This flexibility will allow them to manage their personal and professional lives more harmoniously, fostering a better work-life balance and reducing stress.

In addition to flexibility, resilience can be bolstered through continuous learning opportunities. Generation Alpha values growth and personal development. Providing access to microlearning platforms, online courses, and workshops will not only keep them engaged but also prepare them to adapt to changing job landscapes. Leaders must champion a culture that promotes lifelong learning, making it part of the organisational ethos.

It's equally important to recognise the role of physical health in fostering resilience. Organisations should promote and incentivize physical activity, whether through gym memberships, wellness challenges, or even simple initiatives like standing desks and ergonomic workspace designs. A holistic approach to health will inevitably support better mental well-being, creating a more resilient workforce.

Moreover, fostering a supportive environment means creating spaces where employees can openly share their challenges and successes. Regular team-building activities and social engagements can strengthen bonds and build a supportive network. These could be in the form of virtual coffee breaks or in-person retreats – the key is to create connections.

Another critical aspect of support is leveraging technology to provide real-time feedback. Traditional annual reviews are outdated. Generation Alpha thrives on instant gratification and immediate feedback. Utilising digital tools for continuous performance assessments and development will keep them motivated and aligned with organisational goals.

However, all these strategies depend heavily on leadership. Leaders need to model the behaviour they wish to see. When leaders demonstrate resilience and prioritise mental health, it sets a standard for the entire organisation. This includes maintaining transparency in communication and showing genuine empathy in interactions.

Diversity and inclusion also play pivotal roles in creating a resilient workforce. Organisations need to ensure an environment where every voice is heard and valued. Addressing unconscious biases and fostering an inclusive culture will enable Generation Alpha to bring their authentic selves to work, further enhancing their resilience.

Additionally, recognising and rewarding effort and achievement can significantly boost morale and resilience. Implementing systems where even the smallest of successes are acknowledged can create a positive feedback loop, reinforcing a culture of encouragement and support.

It's also crucial to prepare Generation Alpha for potential challenges and setbacks. Through resilience training workshops, employees can learn coping mechanisms and stress management techniques that will aid them in overcoming hurdles. Encouraging a growth mindset, where failures are seen as learning opportunities, can transform obstacles into developmental milestones.

Lastly, creating a sense of purpose and alignment with larger organisational goals can act as a source of intrinsic motivation. Generation Alpha craves meaning in their work. When they can see the impact of their efforts in real-time and understand how it fits into the bigger picture, it fosters a sense of fulfilment and resilience.

In conclusion, adopting these strategies for support and resilience isn't merely about creating a better work environment; it's about building a future where Generation Alpha can thrive, innovate, and lead. By laying a strong foundation today, we're paving the way for a dynamic and robust workforce that is well-equipped to take on the challenges and opportunities of tomorrow.

The Role of Leaders in Fostering a Healthy Environment isn't just an add-on to leadership; it's the groundwork of a thriving workplace. With Generation Alpha entering the workforce, the role of leaders becomes even more crucial. They will navigate a landscape that demands a blend of traditional wisdom and contemporary agility.

Modern leadership transcends directing tasks and achieving goals. It's about cultivating a space where every team member feels valued, understood, and supported. When leaders prioritise a healthy environment, they set the stage for sustainable success. This involves addressing mental, emotional, and physical well-being, which are all interconnected.

The first step is recognising that well-being is multifaceted. Leaders need to embrace a holistic approach. This means fostering an atmosphere where mental health conversations aren't taboo but encouraged. It's crucial for leaders to destigmatise mental health issues by openly discussing them and ensuring access to resources.

A tangible way for leaders to support mental health is by implementing Employee Assistance Programmes (EAPs). These programmes provide confidential counselling services and mental health resources. By promoting and normalising their use, leaders signal that seeking help is not a sign of weakness but a step towards resilience.

Beyond programmes, the attitudes and behaviours of leaders significantly influence workplace culture. Leaders who demonstrate empathy and emotional intelligence create an environment where employees feel safe to express their concerns. This emotional openness encourages trust and honesty, which are foundational for a healthy workplace.

Leaders have a pivotal role in physical health promotion too. This can be through simple initiatives like encouraging regular breaks, promoting workplace ergonomics, and providing healthy snack options. Work environments that promote physical health can directly impact productivity and overall job satisfaction.

The idea of work-life balance has evolved, and leaders must adapt accordingly. Flexible working arrangements are no longer just perks; they're essential. Offering remote work options, flexible hours, and recognising the importance of personal time off can help employees manage their responsibilities more efficiently.

Technology also plays a significant role in fostering a healthy environment. Tools for remote work, virtual meetings, and online collaboration can make work more adaptable to individual needs. However, leaders must be mindful of the potential for burnout. Encouraging digital detox and respecting boundaries during off-hours can prevent technology-induced stress.

Creating a healthy environment isn't solely about programmes and policies. It's deeply tied to the daily interactions and relationships within a team. Leaders should invest time in understanding the individual needs and preferences of their team members. Regular check-ins, personalised feedback, and genuine interest in their well-being can make a substantial difference.

Learning and development opportunities are another crucial aspect. A culture that encourages continuous growth fosters not just professional development but personal well-being. Leaders should support career progression, skill acquisition, and personal interests.

Recognition and appreciation are powerful tools in a leader's arsenal. Publicly acknowledging achievements, celebrating milestones, and expressing gratitude can boost morale and foster a positive workplace culture. This recognition can come in many forms, from verbal praise to bonuses and awards.

Leaders must also be proactive in creating an inclusive environment. Diversity, Equity, and Inclusion (DEI) initiatives are essential for a healthy workplace. Leaders should champion diversity and ensure that every team member feels seen, heard, and valued. This not only enhances well-being but also drives innovation and creativity.

Accountability is another cornerstone of effective leadership in fostering a healthy environment. Leaders need to hold themselves and their teams accountable for maintaining a respectful and supportive workplace. This includes addressing toxic behaviours promptly and fairly.

Lastly, leaders must model self-care. When leaders take care of their own well-being, they set an example for their teams. Showing that it's okay to take breaks, seek help, and prioritise health encourages employees to do the same.

In conclusion, the role of leaders in fostering a healthy environment is multi-dimensional and dynamic, especially with Generation Alpha stepping into the workforce. By prioritising mental, emotional, and physical well-being, embracing flexibility, promoting growth, and leading by example, leaders can create a thriving workplace where innovation and sustainability are the norms.

Physical Health and Work-Life Balance

Ensuring physical health and maintaining a work-life balance are more important than ever in the age of Generation Alpha, a cohort known for their adaptive prowess and technological fluency. Organisations must prioritise the physical well-being of employees by promoting regular physical activity and providing ergonomic workspaces, whether in-office or remote. Balancing this with flexible work schedules allows employees to better manage personal and professional obligations, reducing burnout and fostering long-term engagement. Such measures not only enhance productivity but also build a culture where well-being is paramount, making the workplace attract and retain top talent from the youngest workforce generation. As we look forward, creating an environment that values health and flexibility will be indispensable for any organisation aiming to thrive in a rapidly evolving landscape.

Encouraging Physical Activity and Ergonomics is not just about making minor adjustments. It's about fostering a comprehensive shift in workplace culture that acknowledges both the physical and mental well-being of Generation Alpha. This cohort, deeply steeped in the digital age, will greatly benefit from environments that counterbalance their inherent tech-savviness with active, ergonomically sound settings.

First and foremost, it's pivotal to recognise that Generation Alpha has been raised in a world where screen time often eclipses physical activity. This creates a unique challenge—and opportunity—for workplaces. By designing thoughtful, activity-friendly spaces and promoting regular movement, employers can help mitigate the sedentary lifestyles that this generation might otherwise lead.

One effective strategy is incorporating "active design" principles into office layouts. This could mean designing workspaces that require minimal movement between different zones or intentionally placing common facilities, like restrooms and break areas, at a distance. The goal here is to encourage incidental physical activity throughout the day.

Beyond layout, consider investing in equipment that promotes movement. Sit-stand desks, for example, offer employees the flexibility to change positions and move around, reducing the risks associated with prolonged sitting. Stability balls and treadmill desks are other options that can be explored to create a more dynamic workspace.

Workplace wellness programs should also have a wide-ranging approach, addressing not just the physical but the mental well-being of employees. Organising group activities, such as yoga or pilates sessions, can foster a sense of community while encouraging physical activity. Participation can be incentivised through small rewards or recognition schemes to boost engagement.

Ergonomics plays a critical role in this equation. Poor ergonomics can lead to discomfort and long-term health issues, reducing productivity and increasing absenteeism. Providing ergonomic assessments and personalised adjustments to workstations can prevent these issues before they arise. This might involve adjustable chairs, monitor stands to ensure screens are at eye level, or even foot rests to support better posture.

Education is key. Employees need to understand the importance of ergonomics and how to implement best practices in their daily routines. Providing training sessions or resources on topics like proper desk setup, posture, and stretching exercises can empower Generation Alpha to take charge of their own health at work.

Moreover, technology should be leveraged to support these initiatives. There are numerous apps and wearables available that can prompt reminders to stand, move around, or take a break. Integrating these tools into the workplace wellness strategy can help make physical activity and ergonomic best practices a seamless part of daily work life.

It's also worth exploring partnerships with fitness centres or wellness providers. Subsidised gym memberships, access to wellness apps, or on-site fitness facilities can provide additional incentives for maintaining an active lifestyle. Tailoring these benefits to appeal to the interests and habits of Generation Alpha can make them more effective.

Let's not overlook the importance of flexibility in work hours and locations, which plays into physical health and ergonomics. Allowing for remote work or flexible scheduling can enable employees to integrate more physical activities into their day, whether that's through home exercise routines or simply having the freedom to take a walking meeting.

In addition, incorporating biophilic design elements—such as natural light, plants, and other elements that connect workers with nature—can significantly enhance physical and mental well-being. Nature has a calming effect and can reduce stress, creating a more inviting and health-focused environment

Physical activity and ergonomics should be seen as ongoing, evolving aspects of workplace culture. Regular feedback from employees can help refine and improve initiatives. Conducting health and wellness surveys can provide insights into what's working and what needs to be adjusted.

Generation Alpha will value employers who demonstrate a commitment to their holistic well-being. This commitment can be a powerful differentiator in attracting and retaining top. talent. By prioritising physical activity and ergonomics, companies signal that they care about their employees beyond just their output.

This commitment is particularly crucial at a time when talent is increasingly demanding more from their employers. Generation Alpha, with their intrinsic understanding of technology and its impacts, will undoubtedly appreciate and expect such progressive stewardship towards their health and well-being in the workplace.

Ultimately, fostering a culture that encourages physical activity and incorporates ergonomic principles is not just about meeting health guidelines; it's about creating a thriving, dynamic workplace that supports the next generation's physical and mental resilience. For forward-thinking leaders and HR professionals, the integration of these habits and principles will be key to nurturing a workforce that's healthy, engaged, and ready to tackle the future.

Flexible Schedules for a Balanced Lifestyle isn't just a trendy phrase; it's a fundamental shift in how we view work and life integration. For Generation Alpha, born into a world where the boundaries between the physical and digital are increasingly blurry, the traditional nine-to-five is an outdated concept. As forward-thinking leaders and HR professionals, it's essential to recognise that flexibility in scheduling isn't merely a perk—it's a necessity.

Consider the profound impact a flexible work schedule can have on an individual's overall well-being. It's not just about the freedom to work when they are most productive, but also the ability to attend to personal and family needs without the stress of being tied to a rigid timetable. This balance fosters resilience, reduces stress levels, and builds a more engaged and committed workforce. Generation Alpha will value employers that understand and respect their time, offering schedules that accommodate various life demands.

The rise of flexible schedules is integral to attracting and retaining top talent from Generation Alpha. This demographic looks for jobs that fit into their lives rather than having to shape their lives around their jobs. If we want to cultivate a sense of loyalty and job satisfaction among these future leaders, adopting flexible work policies is non-negotiable. Companies that cling to outdated models may find themselves at a competitive disadvantage, struggling to engage this emerging workforce.

We can draw lessons from the implementation of flexible schedules in pioneering companies. Take, for example, the tech giants that have embraced flexible hours and remote work long before the global shift caused by the pandemic. By doing so, they have not only attracted top-tier talent but have also seen increases in productivity and innovation. It's clear: when employees are trusted to manage their own schedules, they often rise to the occasion, bringing their best selves to their work.

Creating a balanced lifestyle through flexible scheduling also contributes directly to mental health. When employees can balance work with personal life responsibilities, hobbies, and downtime, they're more likely to maintain a healthier mental state. This is particularly pertinent for Generation Alpha, who will likely face unprecedented levels of digital fatigue and stress from continuous online engagement. A work environment that promotes balance can serve as a safeguard against burnout.

Flexible work schedules also aid in accommodating the diverse working styles and peak productivity times of different individuals. Some people thrive early in the morning, while others hit their stride late at night. By allowing employees to work during their most productive hours, we enable them to perform tasks more efficiently and with higher quality. This customisation boosts overall output and job satisfaction.

Furthermore, flexibility isn't solely about the hours worked; it's also about the autonomy to choose where one works. Remote work, hybrid models, and virtual meeting options enhance the flexibility quotient, giving Generation Alpha the tools they need to work in environments where they feel most comfortable and inspired. It can also bridge the gap for those with long commutes or those living in areas with fewer job opportunities, thus democratizing access to rewarding careers.

Let's not overlook the role flexible schedules play in fostering a diverse workplace. For working parents, caregivers, and individuals with unique personal circumstances, a flexible schedule is more than convenient—it's essential. By embracing this approach, companies make it clear that they are inclusive and considerate of the varied needs of their employees. This inclusivity can lead to a richer, more diverse workplace culture, which in turn drives innovation and empathy.

Strategies for implementing flexible schedules need to be well-thought-out and communicated clearly. Establishing core hours during which everyone is available can help maintain team cohesion and ensure that collaboration isn't hampered. Tools like shared calendars, project management software, and regular check-ins can facilitate effective communication, making sure that flexibility doesn't come at the cost of productivity or connectivity.

We must also consider the importance of establishing boundaries to prevent work from encroaching on personal life. Encouraging employees to unplug after working hours and take regular breaks throughout the day can help sustain long-term productivity and job satisfaction. Leaders should model these behaviours as well, setting a precedent that work-life balance is a top priority.

Of course, flexible schedules present certain challenges, but they are not insurmountable. Potential hurdles such as maintaining team cohesion, ensuring fair distribution of work, and managing performance can be addressed through thoughtful planning and the use of technology. Many companies are already successfully navigating these challenges, proving that flexible scheduling is a viable and sustainable approach.

As you embark on the journey to integrate Generation Alpha into your workplace, remember that flexibility is more than a procedural change; it's a cultural one. The shift towards flexible schedules represents a rethinking of what it means to work effectively and efficiently. It challenges us to trust our employees, to value output over hours logged, and to place well-being at the centre of our organisational practices.

By fostering a balanced lifestyle through flexible schedules, you position your organisation as a forward-thinking, desirable place to work for Generation Alpha. This approach not only benefits the employees but also paves the way for sustainable growth and innovation within the company. In a world that's constantly evolving, flexibility is the key to staying adaptable and resilient.

Ultimately, flexible schedules for a balanced lifestyle aren't just a strategic advantage; they're a commitment to nurturing a healthy, happy, and productive workforce. As we prepare to welcome Generation Alpha, let's embrace this opportunity to reshape the workplace into a space where everyone can thrive, innovate, and grow together.

Chapter 9:
Navigating Legal and
Ethical Landscapes

As we usher Generation Alpha into the workforce, navigating legal and ethical landscapes becomes paramount for leaders and HR professionals. The rise of digital transformation and AI-driven systems brings new complexities in data privacy, security, and ethical decision-making. Companies must spearhead efforts to protect employee information, remaining steadfast in complying with regulations that safeguard privacy. On the frontier of AI and automation, ethical considerations can't be sidelined—balancing efficiency with moral accountability is crucial. Effective governance demands transparency, fostering a culture where decisions are scrutinized through an ethical lens. This dual approach of legal rigour and ethical integrity ensures not just compliance but also builds trust, crucial for creating an inclusive and forward-thinking environment. Empowering our organisations with these principles, we're not only addressing current demands but also setting a benchmark for future generations, fortifying a workplace where innovation thrives within a robust ethical framework.

Data Privacy and Security in the Digital Age

In the ever-evolving digital landscape, protecting data privacy and security has transcended a mere compliance issue to become a critical ethical imperative. As Generation Alpha enters the workforce, raised in a world where digital interactions are second nature, their expectations for data privacy will be unwavering. Organisations need to not only comply with existing regulations but also anticipate and adapt to emerging threats. By employing robust cybersecurity measures and fostering a culture of transparency, companies can build trust and enhance their reputations. This proactive stance not only safeguards sensitive information but also positions organisations as leaders who prioritise ethical considerations in an interconnected world. For forward-thinking leaders, understanding that a commitment to privacy and security is integral to fostering a stable, innovative environment is essential. Combining rigorous data protection protocols with innovative business strategies will not only meet the demands of Generation Alpha but inspire a sense of security and ethical integrity in the workplace.

Protecting Employee Information isn't just a legal necessity; it's a strategic imperative in today's digital world. For those shaping the future of the workplace, particularly with Generation Alpha in mind, safeguarding employee information is foundational to building trust and fostering an environment where innovation and collaboration can thrive.

Generation Alpha, born into a world teeming with technology, views data privacy through a unique lens. They've grown up understanding the value of personal data and the potential risks of its misuse. Hence, they have higher expectations for how organisations manage their information. For forward-thinking leaders, this means not merely complying with regulations but exceeding them, setting new standards for data protection.

First, implement robust data encryption protocols. Generation Alpha employees expect their personal and professional information to be secure not only from external threats but also from internal ones. Use end-to-end encryption to ensure that data transferred between employees and the company's servers is protected. This safeguards against potential breaches that could undermine trust.

Additionally, adopt a zero-trust security model. Unlike traditional security models, a zero-trust approach assumes that threats can come from within as well as outside the network. By continuously verifying access requests, granting the least amount of privilege necessary, and monitoring activities in real-time, organisations can better protect sensitive employee data.

Privacy considerations must extend beyond IT departments. Leaders and HR professionals play a crucial role in embedding a culture of privacy. This means training all employees on best practices in data protection and ensuring they understand the importance of maintaining confidentiality. Generation Alpha, already attuned to the complexities of digital information, will respect and adhere to clear, well-communicated policies.

Transparency is another key element. Generation Alpha prizes openness and will expect to know how their information is being collected, used, and stored. Establish clear privacy policies and make them easily accessible. Regularly update employees about any changes in policies or practices, and involve them in discussions about data protection. This approach builds a culture of trust and mutual respect.

Organisations must also consider the implications of remote work. With the increase in remote and hybrid models, protecting employee information becomes even more challenging yet crucial. Remote work environments can often lack the stringent security measures present in a traditional office, making it imperative to provide employees with secure tools and platforms for communication and collaboration.

Mobile device management (MDM) solutions can help manage and secure employees' mobile devices used for work. These tools can enforce security policies, manage applications, and even wipe data if a device is lost or stolen. Such measures reassure Generation Alpha that their information is protected, regardless of where they are working from.

Next, consider the physical security of data. Paper records, although seemingly outdated, can still pose a significant risk if not properly managed. Implement secure document disposal methods and restrict physical access to areas where sensitive information is stored. Even as digital natives, Generation Alpha will appreciate a comprehensive approach to security that leaves no stone unturned.

A proactive stance on cyber threats is also necessary. Regularly update all software and systems to protect against known vulnerabilities. Conduct frequent security audits and penetration testing to identify and address potential weaknesses. In an age where cybersecurity threats are continually evolving, staying ahead of the curve is essential.

Regulatory compliance must not be overlooked. Adhering to standards such as GDPR, CCPA, or other relevant data protection regulations is non-negotiable. Demonstrating a commitment to these standards will not only protect your organisation from legal repercussions but will also reassure Generation Alpha employees that you are serious about their privacy.

However, compliance is just the starting point. Going beyond regulatory requirements can position your organisation as a leader in data protection. Consider obtaining certifications such as ISO/IEC 27001, which demonstrates adherence to global best practices in information security management.

The ethical handling of employee data is another important consideration. Balances need to be struck between data utilisation and privacy. Avoid unnecessary data collection and ensure that any data collected is used responsibly and ethically. Clearly define and limit access to employee data to only those who truly need it for their roles.

In the event of a data breach, having a robust incident response plan is critical. This plan should detail steps for immediate action to contain and mitigate the breach, communication strategies for informing affected parties, and measures for preventing future incidents. Swift and transparent communication during a breach can significantly lessen the impact on employee trust.

By taking these steps, organisations can protect employee information effectively, meeting and exceeding the expectations of Generation Alpha. This approach not only safeguards individual privacy but also enhances the overall trust and cohesion within the workplace, laying a strong foundation for future innovation and success.

Regulations and Compliance have never been more critical or more complex, especially as we prepare to integrate Generation Alpha into the workplace. Forward-thinking leaders, HR professionals, and strategists must navigate an evolving landscape of rules and standards that will ensure fair treatment, safety, and equal opportunities for this new cohort.

The first aspect to consider is data privacy and security. Generation Alpha, born into a digital world, expects and demands rigorous protection of their personal information. With regulations like GDPR and CCPA setting the benchmark, companies have a legal and ethical obligation to implement robust data security measures. It's not just about compliance—it's about building trust with a generation that values their digital footprint.

Additionally, transparency will be a significant expectation. Generation Alpha has grown up in an environment where information is often just a click away. They will push for clear and direct communication about how their data is being used and protected. Employers must be prepared to provide detailed explanations and be swift in addressing any concerns or breaches.

Environmental regulations are another substantial area of focus. Given Generation Alpha's strong ties to sustainability, companies need to comply with existing environmental laws and anticipate more stringent regulations in the future. This might include adhering to carbon emission standards, investing in renewable energy, and committing to sustainable supply chains.

Employee health and safety regulations are also evolving. The recent pandemic has catalysed changes in how we approach workplace safety and wellness. Companies must adapt to these new norms by ensuring flexible work policies, ergonomic workspaces, and health-focused programmes that meet the regulatory standards while addressing the unique needs of Generation Alpha. This includes mental health provisions, which are increasingly becoming mandated in workplace regulations.

Another critical aspect of compliance is in the realm of diversity, equity, and inclusion (DEI). Global regulations are tightening around ensuring that workplaces are genuinely inclusive. Leaders will need to go beyond merely following anti-discrimination laws—they'll have to proactively foster an inclusive culture that values diversity. This involves equitable hiring practices, continuous DEI training, and creating an environment where all employees feel valued and heard.

As automation and AI integrations become commonplace, ethical considerations come into sharp focus. Regulations around AI are in their nascent stages, but it's clear that companies will need to develop ethical frameworks to govern AI use. This includes ensuring transparency in AI-driven decisions, preventing algorithmic biases, and protecting jobs from becoming entirely automated without alternative roles being created.

Work hours and fair compensation regulations will also require attention. With Generation Alpha valuing work-life balance, companies will need to comply with laws around minimum wages, overtime pay, and fair working hours. Flexible working policies that are compliant with labour laws will be essential to attract and retain this new workforce.

Training and development regulations are another essential part of the compliance landscape. As the necessity for continuous learning grows, regulations are being introduced to ensure that employees receive adequate training opportunities. Companies must offer programmes that not only comply with these regulations but also align with the career aspirations of Generation Alpha.

Intellectual property rights will be more pertinent as Generation Alpha brings fresh ideas and innovations. Companies must navigate the tricky waters of IP regulations to ensure that they are protecting their own innovations while respecting the intellectual property of others. This also includes educating Generation Alpha about these regulations so they understand the importance of protecting their creative output.

Furthermore, companies must prepare for global compliance challenges, especially if they operate in multiple jurisdictions. Compliance with international labour laws, tax regulations, and business practices will be crucial. This requires a comprehensive understanding of various global standards and the ability to adapt swiftly to new regulations as they arise.

Employee benefits, such as health insurance and retirement plans, must also align with regulatory standards. As Generation Alpha enters the workforce, they will be looking at benefits packages that not only meet their current needs but also offer long-term security. Ensuring compliance with both statutory and voluntary benefit regulations will be key in this aspect.

Companies must also gear up to meet the increasing legal requirements around remote work. Regulations concerning remote work are still evolving, but it's evident that companies will need to establish clear policies that comply with local labour laws while offering the flexibility that Generation Alpha seeks. This includes addressing issues related to remote work compensation, health and safety, and data security.

Finally, companies need to stay ahead with continuous risk assessments and audits to ensure compliance. By regularly reviewing policies, procedures, and practices, they can make necessary adjustments to align with changing regulations and Generation Alpha's expectations. This proactive approach not only mitigates risks but also positions companies as responsible and forward-thinking employers.

In conclusion, **Regulations and Compliance** are foundational elements in integrating Generation Alpha into the workplace. Leaders must embrace this dynamic regulatory landscape, understanding that compliance is not a one-time effort but a continuous, evolving process. By doing so, they will not only meet legal obligations but also build a workplace that resonates with the values and expectations of the upcoming generation.

Ethical Considerations in AI and Automation

Balancing the rapid advance of AI and automation with ethical responsibilities is crucial for organisations aiming to integrate Generation Alpha into the workplace. As we stand at the cusp of unprecedented technological growth, it's vital that we consider the moral implications of these advancements. Not only must we ensure transparency and accountability in decision-making processes, but we must also address the potential impact on employment and job security. Incorporating AI doesn't just mean better efficiency; it demands a reevaluation of our ethical frameworks to prevent unintended consequences. By fostering a culture of ethical innovation, leaders can promote both technological progress and social responsibility, ultimately creating an environment where humanity and technology coexist harmoniously. Remember, the goal isn't to replace human intuition and creativity, but to augment them in ways that uphold our core values and propel us toward a brighter, more equitable future.

Balancing Efficiency with Ethical Responsibilities has never been more crucial than in today's rapidly evolving workplace environment. As businesses grapple with integrating advanced technologies like AI and automation, they must also navigate the moral landscape these innovations entail. The pursuit of efficiency should not eclipse the imperative to engage ethically with both employees and the wider community. In the context of preparing for Generation Alpha, achieving this balance demands a nuanced approach that recognises the unique values and expectations of this digital-native cohort.

Generation Alpha, born from 2010 onwards, has grown up with technology seamlessly woven into their daily lives. While this technological proficiency suggests that they will likely drive and welcome efficiency-enhancing innovations, it also implies a heightened expectation for ethical considerations in how these technologies are deployed. For organisations, this means embedding ethical frameworks into their operational strategies, ensuring that speed and efficiency do not come at the cost of fairness and justice.

This emerging generation is acutely aware of issues like data privacy, environmental sustainability, and social justice. Therefore, we need to ask ourselves: How do we introduce AI and automation, which are often designed to optimise efficiency, without compromising ethical standards? The answer lies in creating a symbiotic relationship between technological tools and ethical guidelines, ensuring that advancements serve the broader good while respecting individual rights and societal norms.

Transparency is paramount in sustaining this balance. Clear communication regarding the use of AI and automated processes can help assuage fears and misconceptions. Employees should be well-informed about how these technologies impact their roles and workloads. Transparency also extends to the decision-making processes embedded within AI systems. By elucidating how decisions are made and on what basis, organisations can foster trust and mitigate the anxiety that often accompanies technological change.

Another critical aspect involves accountability. As organisations leverage AI for various operational efficiencies, it becomes essential to establish robust accountability mechanisms. Who is responsible when an AI system makes a flawed decision? How are these systems trained and maintained, and by whom? These questions need concrete answers, underpinned by a commitment to ethical responsibility. Establishing clear lines of accountability ensures that when things go awry, there is a structured way to address and rectify issues.

Moreover, focusing on ethical AI usage isn't just about addressing risks; it's about seizing opportunities for positive impact. When ethical considerations are incorporated into the design and implementation of technology, it can lead to more inclusive and equitable workplaces. For example, AI can be utilised to reduce human biases in recruitment processes, ensuring a more diverse and qualified talent pool. By investing in ethical AI, organisations not only safeguard against potential pitfalls but also enhance their reputation and inclusivity.

Generation Alpha is also highly attuned to the societal impacts of corporate actions. They expect companies to take stances on social issues and to act responsibly. This extends to how businesses deploy technology. Employing ethical AI and automation strategies exemplifies a company's commitment to these principles. For instance, ensuring that AI-driven decisions do not perpetuate stereotypes or biases aligns with Generation Alpha's values of inclusivity and fairness. It's about more than just avoiding harm; it's about actively contributing to a just and equitable society.

Furthermore, as businesses adopt new technologies, they must ensure that these tools are improving rather than diminishing employee well-being. Automation should relieve humans of repetitive tasks, not replace human ingenuity or reduce job quality. This balance requires regular feedback mechanisms where employees can voice concerns about the impacts of new technologies on their work conditions. By listening to their workforce, organisations can make necessary adjustments that align efficiency with well-being, making work more fulfilling and less stressful.

Training and education play critical roles in this balancing act. Employees need to be equipped with the skills to work alongside advanced technologies, and this training must emphasise ethical considerations as much as operational efficiency. A well-rounded approach that incorporates both hard and soft skills – technical competency and ethical reasoning – prepares the workforce to thrive in an evolving landscape while upholding high moral standards.

In integrating Generation Alpha, businesses must be adaptive and proactive. This means continuously re-evaluating and updating their ethical frameworks in response to new technological developments. It's not a one-time initiative but an ongoing commitment. By fostering a culture that prioritises ethics alongside efficiency, companies can navigate the complexities of modern technology with integrity and purpose.

Involving Generation Alpha in decision-making processes also promotes ethical responsibility. As digital natives, they can offer fresh perspectives on how technologies should be utilised and what ethical safeguards should be in place. Their input can be invaluable in ensuring that technological integration aligns with contemporary ethical standards and expectations. Engaging them not only leverages their insights but also demonstrates respect for their values, fostering a more inclusive and forward-thinking workplace culture.

Moreover, companies should look beyond internal policies and consider their broader impact on society. This entails advocating for responsible AI use industry-wide and supporting policies and initiatives that promote ethical innovation. By taking a leadership role in these conversations, businesses can influence the larger ecosystem, driving progress toward a future where technology serves humanity responsibly and equitably.

The focus on balancing efficiency with ethical responsibilities ultimately contributes to building trust – both within the organisation and with external stakeholders. When employees see that their employers prioritise ethical considerations, it fosters loyalty and engagement. Similarly, when customers and clients perceive a company as ethically responsible, it enhances the brand's reputation and builds trust.

Ethical technology use is not just about meeting regulatory requirements; it's about exemplifying leadership in a new era defined by rapid technological advancement and profound social change. By championing ethics as foundational to innovation and efficiency, businesses position themselves as leaders in the transition to a future marked by both technological prowess and moral integrity.

It's clear that the integration of Generation Alpha into the workplace requires a delicate balance between harnessing the efficiencies offered by emerging technologies and upholding steadfast ethical standards. This balance, though challenging, is not only possible but also essential for creating sustainable, inclusive, and innovative workplaces. By committing to this equilibrium, organisations can effectively merge progress with principle, ensuring that the future of work is both efficient and ethically sound.

Transparency and Accountability in Decision Making are not mere buzzwords for companies aiming to appeal to Generation Alpha; they're prerequisites for gaining trust and fostering an environment of mutual respect. This cohort, growing up in an era where information is readily accessible and instantly shareable, places an unparalleled emphasis on openness. Hidden agendas and opaque processes? They won't fly here.

First off, let's talk transparency. For Generation Alpha, the idea of a closed-door meeting feels outdated. They crave insight into the decision-making processes that affect their roles and the broader organisational trajectory. This generation grew up watching YouTube tutorials that peel back the curtain on everything from making gourmet meals to coding video games. They're conditioned to expect full disclosure. So, why should the workplace be any different?

Consider the benefits of transparency. When decisions are made openly, it helps dispel any lingering suspicion about hidden motives. Employees become more accepting of outcomes—even those they might initially disagree with—because they understand the thought process and criteria involved. This clarity ensures everyone is on the same page and reduces the likelihood of misunderstandings that can derail productivity.

Now, how do organisations achieve this level of transparency? One effective method is the use of open forums or town hall meetings, where employees at all levels can ask questions and receive real-time answers. This isn't just about offering a stage for upper management; it's about creating a dialogue. Leaders who regularly engage openly with their teams build a reservoir of goodwill and trust that's invaluable, especially during challenging times.

Transparency also applies to the information flow within the company. Share the 'why' behind goals and decisions, not just the 'what'. Whether it's through detailed project reports, open-access databases for non-sensitive information, or even regular updates on business performance, the idea is to make information accessible for those who seek it. Remember, an informed workforce is an empowered one.

Accountability is the other side of the coin. For Generation Alpha, accountability is about holding people responsible for their actions, ensuring they deliver on their promises and uphold ethical standards. Leaders must model this behaviour, showing that accountability starts at the top. When employees see leaders who freely admit their mistakes and take steps to rectify them, it sets a powerful example.

One practical approach is setting up clearly defined metrics and KPIs that are linked to both team and individual performance. These benchmarks should be transparent and available for everyone to review. Automated tools can help in this regard by tracking progress in real-time, making the data readily accessible and ensuring that everyone understands what success looks like. It's not about micromanagement but about fostering a sense of shared responsibility.

Furthermore, peer reviews can add another layer of accountability. When employees evaluate each other, it not only provides a more comprehensive performance assessment but also builds a community of trust and mutual accountability. Generation Alpha, with their emphasis on collaboration and collective success, will likely thrive in such an environment.

Accountability also involves ethical decision-making. The rise of artificial intelligence and automated processes brings new ethical challenges. Leaders must ensure these technologies are used responsibly, balancing efficiency with ethical considerations. This means establishing guidelines and protocols for AI usage and regularly auditing these systems to ensure they're aligned with the company's ethical standards.

Remember that ethical accountability isn't just about compliance with regulations; it's about doing the right thing even when it's difficult. This includes being upfront about potential downsides to new technologies or business decisions. Employees, especially those from Generation Alpha, respect leaders who can be candid about challenges and committed to finding solutions that benefit the community, not just the bottom line.

Accountability mechanisms should also include feedback loops from employees. Creating a culture where feedback is not just accepted but actively solicited can lead to significant improvements in decision-making processes. When employees feel their opinions matter, they are more likely to take ownership of projects and contribute to a positive work culture.

The integration of transparency and accountability doesn't just benefit employees—it strengthens the entire organisation. It leads to better decision-making, increased innovation, and a more resilient workforce. Companies that successfully embed these principles into their cultures will not just attract top talent from Generation Alpha but retain them.

One can argue that transparency and accountability pave the way for a more democratic workplace. But it's more than that; it's about fostering a sense of belonging and purpose. When employees understand the 'why' behind their work and see that their leaders are accountable, they're not just working for a paycheck. They're part of a mission.

In an age where information flows freely and swiftly, and where ethical considerations are under more scrutiny than ever, ensuring transparency and accountability in decision-making isn't just a competitive advantage—it's a necessity. As we prepare for Generation Alpha's entry into the workforce, let's aim to build workplaces that are open, honest, and responsible. This is how we'll foster a culture where innovation, flexibility, and sustainability truly thrive.

Chapter 10:
Preparing for the Unpredictable

In an era where change is the only constant, preparing for the unpredictable requires more than just a vision; it demands agility, innovation, and a resilient mindset. For forward-thinking leaders, HR professionals, and strategists, embracing uncertainty is not a choice but a necessity. Scenario planning and agile methodologies enable organisations to adapt swiftly and efficiently, fostering a culture where collab-oration and experimentation are the norms rather than exceptions. By encouraging teams to learn from both successes and failures, we cultivate an environment of continuous improvement. It's about building resilience not just in systems and processes, but in people, empowering them to thrive amid volatility. As Generation Alpha enters the workplace, their innate ability to navigate digital landscapes and demand for social responsibility will challenge us to rethink our approaches continually. Our goal is to create workplaces that don't just survive but prosper through uncertainty, leveraging innovation to turn unpredictability into opportunity.

Scenario Planning and Agile Methodologies

In a world where the only constant is change, mastering scenario planning and agile methodologies becomes indispensable. These tools allow organisations to not just prepare for the future but to actively shape it. Scenario planning challenges leaders to consider multiple potential outcomes and unmet needs, fostering a proactive rather than reactive approach. Coupling this with agile methodologies, teams can swiftly adapt to unforeseen challenges and leverage new opportunities. It's about creating a culture unafraid of pivots and bold enough to experiment with innovative solutions. By embracing these practices, leaders can cultivate resilience and responsiveness, essential traits as we integrate Generation Alpha into the workplace. Providing a framework for continuous learning and flexibility, it's clear that the road ahead requires these dynamic strategies to navigate future complexities confidently.

Adapting to Change in Uncertain Times in today's rapidly shifting landscape isn't just a buzzphrase; it's a necessity. Especially when we think about the introduction of Generation Alpha into the workforce. This demographic, shaped by technological advances and unique societal challenges, compels business leaders, HR professionals, and strategists to rethink normatives and adapt swiftly. But how do we navigate this ever-changing terrain?

First and foremost, understanding the significance of agility is paramount. Organisations used to take years to adjust to new technologies or market changes, but now, they need to pivot within months—or even weeks. Generation Alpha, with their innate digital prowess, will expect employers to keep up with the pace of technological advancements. This necessitates a dynamic approach to both management and operational strategies.

However, it's not just about speed. Adaptability involves a profound mindset shift, embracing a culture where change is not only expected but welcomed. For Generation Alpha, accustomed to the constant evolution of digital platforms and social paradigms, flexibility must be embedded into the organisational DNA. Companies that resist this cultural shift risk becoming obsolete, losing out on attracting the best young talent.

Another pivotal aspect is the development of a robust, adaptable workforce. Here's where continuous learning plays a critical role. Traditional education models are no longer sufficient. Organisations must promote lifelong learning and provide platforms for constant skill enhancement. Microlearning and online courses offer immediate application of new skills, aligning with Generation Alpha's learning preferences and the need for immediate relevance.

Corporate structures also need to transform. Command-and-control hierarchies may hinder the innovative spirit Generation Alpha brings. Instead, fostering networks where ideas flow freely and collaboration is encouraged can create an environment ripe for innovation. This shift towards network-based operations will enhance overall agility and responsiveness.

The role of leadership also evolves in uncertain times. Leaders must be more than decision-makers; they should act as facilitators of change, guiding their teams through turbulence with empathy and vision. Emotional intelligence becomes a critical leadership trait, helping to build trust and resilience within teams. For Generation Alpha, leaders who demonstrate these qualities will resonate deeply, establishing a bridge between the company's mission and the workforce's values.

Strategic planning remains vital but must be more flexible than ever. Traditional long-term planning cycles are increasingly giving way to agile methodologies that allow for rapid iteration and course correction. Scenario planning becomes an essential tool, offering multiple futures preparedness. By anticipating a range of potential outcomes, organisations can remain resilient and adaptive, ready to pivot as needed.

Innovation is often born from necessity, and times of uncertainty can be fertile grounds for creative solutions. Encouraging risk-taking within the organisation is crucial. Generation Alpha, unencumbered by traditional failure stigmas, is likely to respond positively to environments where experimentation is valued. Recognising and rewarding innovative efforts, regardless of the outcome, helps to instil a culture where bold ideas flourish.

Collaboration across diverse teams can also fuel adaptability. Drawing insights from a wide range of perspectives not only enriches problem-solving capacity but fosters inclusivity. Generation Alpha, growing up in a more globally connected world, will expect this diversity as standard. It's essential to leverage these varied viewpoints to navigate the unpredictability of the business landscape successfully.

Technological integration is another area where adaptability is paramount. The rapid evolution of AI, blockchain, and virtual reality means companies must continually reassess their tech infrastructure. For Generation Alpha, seamless integration of these technologies into the workplace will be a baseline expectation. Hence, a proactive approach to adopting and scaling new tech solutions is critical.

Yet, amid all these adaptations, maintaining a focus on ethical considerations remains essential. Transparency in decision-making, particularly when deploying emerging technologies, builds trust within the organisation and with external stakeholders. Generation Alpha values ethical responsibility highly, and businesses must weave this into their operational ethos to stay aligned with these new workforce entrants.

It's easy to get caught up in the chaos of constant change, but organisations must also pay attention to the wellness of their employees. Balance and well-being cannot be sacrificed on the altar of adaptation. Implementing flexible work schedules and promoting work-life balance are not just perks but necessities in retaining a happy, productive workforce. Generation Alpha views these elements as fundamental to their job satisfaction and overall health.

The agility required to navigate uncertain times effectively extends to the very core of corporate strategies. This means constantly iterating on company policies, staying ahead of legal requirements, and ensuring that ethical considerations guide every decision. Adaptability isn't just a strategy; it's a continuous, evolving process that must be nurtured within the fabric of the company.

Lastly, it's about fostering a future-oriented mindset. Preparedness for uncertainty involves cultivating an organisational culture that's inherently forward-looking. Generation Alpha, naturally attuned to rapid changes and new possibilities, can drive this perspective with their fresh, innovative approaches. Embracing this mindset harnesses their potential and positions the company as a leader in an ever-evolving market.

In conclusion, adapting to change in uncertain times isn't merely about reacting to external forces. It's a holistic approach that encompasses cultural shifts, leadership evolution, constant learning, and ethical integrity. By embracing these elements, organisations can not only survive but thrive, ushering in a future where Generation Alpha can lead the way toward continued innovation and success.

Resilience and Recovery Strategies are no longer just buzzwords; they are imperative for enduring success in a rapidly changing world. As forward-thinking leaders, HR professionals, and strategists, you're likely already aware of the volatile environment that defines today's business landscape. One critical factor to consider is the impending arrival of Generation Alpha into the workforce. The exceptional diversity, digital proficiency, and social consciousness of this generation make it essential to hone resilience and formulate robust recovery strategies.

Before diving into specific strategies, let's ground ourselves in the context. Traditional risk management approaches won't suffice when dealing with the complexities brought by Gen Alpha. The digital-

151

native generation will face issues such as cyber threats more frequently and with greater intensity. Therefore, we need a multi-faceted approach that caters to both existing and emerging needs.

First and foremost, resilience must begin with a robust organisational culture. A culture that celebrates adaptability, encourages continuous learning, and values emotional well-being builds a workforce that can weather any storm. Creating this type of environment involves fostering trust and open communication channels. When team members feel valued and heard, they are far more likely to adapt quickly and effectively to change.

But what does this look like in practice? Start with simple yet powerful steps like regular check-ins and transparent, empathetic leadership. Open the floor for employees to voice concerns and suggest solutions. Create an atmosphere where making mistakes is not just accepted but seen as an essential part of the learning curve. Gen Alpha, in particular, thrives in environments that celebrate innovation and iterative learning.

Building resilience also extends to technical infrastructure. The future workplace must be equipped with state-of-the-art security measures and robust contingency plans. From secure cloud storage solutions to well-defined data recovery protocols, having these mechanisms in place mitigates risks and ensures business continuity. Furthermore, incorporating AI and machine learning can help anticipate and mitigate potential threats before they become significant issues.

A comprehensive approach to resilience also entails diversifying skill sets within your workforce. Today's dynamic job market values multi-skilled employees who can pivot across various roles when needed. Gen Alpha's comfort with digital tools and platforms makes them uniquely suited for cross-disciplinary roles. Encourage ongoing professional development through workshops, certifications, and courses. The more varied the skills within your team, the better prepared you'll be to tackle unforeseen challenges.

Now, let's talk about recovery strategies. While resilience focuses on preparation and mitigation, recovery concerns post-incident actions that restore normalcy. A well-thought-out recovery plan should span multiple layers — from individual employee well-being to full organisational revival.

A multi-tiered approach begins on the personal level. Offer mental health support, flexible work arrangements, and opportunities for relaxation and recreation. Gen Alpha values a work-life balance and mental wellness more than previous generations, making this a critical component in your recovery strategy. Mind you, these aren't perks but necessities in today's work environment. Initiatives like these contribute significantly to quick and effective recovery by ensuring that your workforce remains motivated and engaged.

At an organisational level, recovery strategies should include clear, actionable steps for restoring operations. Conduct regular crisis management simulations to keep your team prepared and efficient. Create recovery "teams" with specific roles so everyone knows what to do when a crisis strikes. Believe it or not, such measures drastically reduce downtime and operational hiccups.

One effective tactic is to establish a dedicated "resilience officer" or a similar role focused on navigating crises, implementing recovery strategies, and continually refining these processes. This role should work closely with leadership and HR to assess vulnerabilities, monitor ongoing risks, and develop tailored training programs.

Technology plays a pivotal role here as well. Leverage digital platforms for real-time communication and decision-making during crises. Use AI-driven tools for rapid assessment and data analysis, providing you with the agility to make informed decisions quickly.

These tools are not just efficient but also scalable, making them particularly useful for companies anticipating significant growth or geographical expansion.

You might wonder how to defend resource allocation for resilience and recovery initiatives. The answer lies in the long-term returns. Companies that are resilient and have strong recovery plans can bounce back faster, maintaining client trust and market reputation. This is not just futures thinking; it's practical strategy grounded in a proven track record. Consider these investments as a form of long-term insurance, safeguarding both financial performance and organisational integrity.

The next step is ensuring that your recovery strategies align with your broader business objectives. Every plan should be backed by metrics to measure its effectiveness. Use KPIs such as "time to recovery," "employee morale post-crisis," and "client retention rates" to gauge your success. Continually refine these plans based on feedback and real-world outcomes.

In summary, cultivating resilience and executing efficient recovery strategies are key to integrating Generation Alpha into the workforce. These approaches not only fortify your organisation but also leverage the unique strengths and preferences of this new generation. By combining strong organisational culture, technical infrastructure, diversified skills, and comprehensive plans, you're setting your company up for sustained success in a rapidly evolving world.

It's clear that tomorrow's leaders will need to be more agile, more empathetic, and more tech-savvy than ever before. By focusing on resilience and recovery, you're not just preparing for the unpredictable; you're embracing a sustainable approach to leadership that benefits everyone involved. The journey may be challenging, but the rewards are immense — not just for your organisation but for the broader societal landscape as well.

Fostering a Culture of Innovation and Adaptability

In the face of uncertainty, fostering a culture of innovation and adaptability isn't just a nice-to-have; it's essential for survival and growth. As we prepare our organisations for the unpredictability that comes with integrating Generation Alpha into the workplace, it's crucial to cultivate an environment where creativity and flexibility are not only encouraged but ingrained in the corporate ethos. This means embracing a mindset that values experimentation, rewards risk-taking, and sees failure as an opportunity to learn and evolve. Leaders must champion these values and create structures that support rapid iteration and agile responses to change. Whether it's through interdisciplinary collaboration or implementing feedback loops for continuous improvement, the ability to pivot and adapt will define the organisations that thrive in this next era. Let's equip ourselves with the strategies and tools that make dynamic innovation second nature, setting the stage for a resilient and forward-thinking future.

Encouraging Collaboration and Experimentation is not just a strategic move for the modern workplace; it's a necessity. In a world that's constantly evolving, businesses need to foster an environment where new ideas can thrive, and collaboration is at the heart of innovation. For Generation Alpha, who are growing up in a much more interconnected and fast-paced world, the emphasis on teamwork and creativity will be more critical than ever.

First and foremost, Generation Alpha will bring a fresh perspective to the workplace. They're digital natives, comfortable with technology in ways previous generations couldn't even fathom. Leveraging their tech-savviness to promote collaboration can yield astounding results. Digital collaboration tools, from project management software to real-time communication platforms, will become second nature to them. By ensuring these tools are integrated seamlessly into the work

155

environment, organisations can empower employees to work together more efficiently than ever before.

However, collaboration isn't just about tools—it's about culture. Cultivating a culture that celebrates team achievements, values diverse input, and promotes open communication can inspire employees to work together more effectively. For Generation Alpha, who value transparency and ethical practices, creating such an inclusive culture will be crucial. Teams that feel valued and heard are more likely to take intellectual risks, which can lead to groundbreaking innovations.

Encouraging experimentation goes hand in hand with fostering collaboration. It's essential to create safe spaces where employees can test new ideas without the fear of failure. This means leaders need to be open to unconventional approaches and ready to support 'failures' as opportunities for learning and growth. Providing time and resources for employees to pursue side projects or 'innovation sprints' can lead to unexpected breakthroughs.

Incorporating Design Thinking

One practical way to encourage experimentation is by incorporating design thinking principles into daily operations. Design thinking focuses on understanding user needs, prototyping, and iterating on solutions. This methodology not only fosters creativity but also validates ideas through user-centric testing. Generation Alpha, with their user-first mindset and natural inclination towards empathy, will excel in environments that embrace such an iterative process.

Creating cross-functional teams is another effective strategy. By bringing together individuals with diverse skill sets and backgrounds, businesses can generate a wide array of ideas and perspectives. Cross-functional collaboration fosters a holistic approach to problem-solving, ensuring that solutions are innovative and well-rounded.

Encouraging these teams to work in agile sprints can further enhance productivity and innovation.

Leadership's Role

Leadership plays a pivotal role in fostering a culture of collaboration and experimentation. Leaders need to model collaborative behaviour and actively participate in team activities. Transparent decision-making and open-door policies can also contribute to a more inclusive and collaborative environment. Recognising and rewarding teamwork, rather than just individual achievements, can reinforce the importance of collaboration.

It's also crucial for leaders to remain adaptable and open-minded. Encouraging a growth mindset throughout the organisation can help employees feel more comfortable experimenting and adapting to new methodologies. Generation Alpha leaders, in particular, need to focus on emotional intelligence and empathy to effectively lead diverse and dynamic teams.

Creating Incentives

Incentives can drive collaboration and experimentation. Simple reward systems that recognise both team and individual contributions to innovative projects can be highly effective. Whether it's through monetary bonuses, extra time off, or public recognition, showing appreciation for employees who collaborate and experiment can serve as a powerful motivator.

Flexible work environments that provide time for personal projects and professional development can also encourage experimentation. Allocating a few hours each week for employees to explore new ideas or collaborate on side projects can yield surprising innovations. This flexibility shows employees that the organisation values creativity and continuous improvement.

Utilising Collaborative Technologies

Tech will play a significant role in facilitating collaboration and experimentation for Generation Alpha. Cloud-based platforms, shared digital workspaces, and virtual reality meeting rooms can bring teams together in ways that were previously deemed impossible. Integrating AI technologies to assist in project management can further streamline team efforts, making the collaborative process even more efficient.

Providing training on these technologies ensures that all employees, regardless of their tech-savviness, can contribute effectively. Generation Alpha's comfort with digital tools can be an asset here, as they can often act as tech mentors, helping others navigate new platforms and systems with ease.

Learning from Failures

Failure needs to be reframed as a learning opportunity. By creating a blame-free environment where employees can openly discuss what went wrong and what could be improved, organisations can cultivate a culture of continuous learning and improvement. Post-mortem meetings and after-action reviews can be invaluable tools for this purpose.

Encouraging an iterative approach, where employees are guided through cycles of planning, testing, and feedback, can demystify the process of experimentation. When failures are approached as a crucial part of the innovation process, teams can move forward with more confidence and resilience.

Encouraging Diversity of Thought

Diversity of thought is at the core of successful collaboration and experimentation. Organisations need to actively seek diverse perspectives by fostering an inclusive environment where every voice is heard. This involves not only hiring a diverse workforce but also encouraging diversity in project teams and idea generation sessions.

Workshops and brainstorming sessions that encourage out-of-the-box thinking can also stimulate creativity and innovation. These sessions should be structured to ensure everyone's ideas are considered and valued. Setting up 'innovation labs' where employees can experiment with new concepts in a low-risk environment can further drive a culture of innovation.

The Role of Physical Spaces

Physical workspaces that foster collaboration and creativity can make a huge difference. Open-plan offices, collaborative zones, and quiet spaces for focused work cater to various working styles and needs. Comfortable, flexible spaces that encourage spontaneous interactions can lead to serendipitous innovations.

For many organisations, investing in spaces that inspire creativity is just as important as investing in digital tools. Spaces designed to be adaptable can easily be reconfigured to suit different types of collaborative work, from brainstorming sessions to project sprints.

Leveraging External Networks

Encouraging collaboration and experimentation doesn't have to be confined within the walls of your organisation. Leveraging external networks, such as partnerships with startups, academic institutions, and industry groups, can bring in fresh perspectives and expertise.

These collaborations can lead to innovative joint ventures and dynamic problem-solving approaches.

Hosting hackathons, innovation challenges, and workshops with external participants can also infuse new energy and ideas into your organisation. These events can spark creativity and drive forward-thinking solutions that may not have been considered internally.

The journey to encourage collaboration and experimentation is ongoing and ever-evolving. The arrival of Generation Alpha presents a unique opportunity to redefine how we work together and innovate. By embracing their strengths and building an environment that supports collaboration and experimentation, organisations can unlock unprecedented potential and shape the future of work.

Learning from Failures and Successes in the context of preparing for Generation Alpha's integration into the workplace is more than just a notion; it's a foundational pillar of innovative thinking. This generation, having grown up in a whirlwind of technological advancements and global shifts, possesses unique expectations and demands. Understanding their preferences requires us to examine not only our triumphs but also our missteps.

First, let's acknowledge that the failures we've encountered in dealing with previous generations provide invaluable lessons. In asking ourselves where we went wrong, we uncover blind spots in organisational culture, leadership styles, and communication methods. For instance, Generation Alpha will soon demand workplaces that are not only digitally equipped but also empathetically led. Past experiences with Millennials and Gen Z illustrate the critical importance of adaptability and inclusivity, two areas where failures can quickly become powerful learning experiences.

Consider the notorious example of rigid hierarchical structures that stifled innovation. These structures are fading in favour of networks that foster collaboration and creative freedom. Generation Alpha will push this trend even further, seeking leaders who are mentors rather than commanders. Past failures in adopting such leadership models highlight the urgency of continual evolution in management practices. If organisations have been slow to abandon outdated hierarchal systems, they must navigate this transition seamlessly to appeal to Generation Alpha.

Equally important is the necessity to learn from successes. Businesses that have thrived amid rapid technological advancement often share common virtues: agility, creativity, and a deep-rooted culture of continuous learning. These qualities align closely with Generation Alpha's attributes and can serve as blueprints for future success. By examining what worked well, organisations can replicate and refine these strategies to meet the evolving needs of new generations.

For example, companies like Google and Spotify excel because they continually invest in their employees' professional development. The culture of learning prevalent at such organisations reinforces the value of curiosity and lifelong learning, traits Generation Alpha holds dear. By investing in a learning culture now, firms can not only attract but also retain the talent of tomorrow.

Another crucial aspect is embracing a culture that views failure not as a setback but as a stepping stone for success. Organisations that promote risk-taking, albeit measured and informed, stand to gain significantly. Failures should be dissected to extract insights that lead to better approaches and solutions. This mindset is particularly relevant in a fast-evolving environment, where Generation Alpha will expect rapid, responsive, and transparent organisational behaviour.

Yet, discussing learning from failure would be incomplete without mentioning resilience. Resilience is the underlying strength that allows organisations to bounce back, adapt, and thrive amidst setbacks.

Building a resilient workplace can involve multiple strategies, such as fostering strong internal communications, promoting diversity and inclusion, and ensuring that mental and physical well-being is prioritised. These are strategies that past experiences have shown to be effective and crucial for a robust organisational foundation.

Learning from successes, on the other hand, involves an equally nuanced approach. Successful integration of new technologies, for example, offers clues about effective change management practices. We understand that implementation is most successful when end-users— our employees—are involved in the conversation. Evaluating what has worked in these implementations provides a framework to introduce future technologies seamlessly, ensuring that Generation Alpha feels both engaged and empowered.

Another avenue worth exploring is the role of mentorship programs. Organisations that have successfully implemented ment- orship and reverse-mentorship programs create a flow of knowledge that benefits all parties involved. For Generation Alpha, mentorship will likely be one of the key factors in workplace satisfaction. Reverse- mentorship, on the other hand, can provide senior employees with fresh perspectives on emerging trends and technologies, bridging the generational divide.

Failures also offer critical insights when addressing sustainability and corporate social responsibility (CSR). Generation Alpha, raised with a keen awareness of environmental and social issues, expects organisations to act responsibly. Missteps in this domain can be unforgiving. Therefore, it is crucial to revisit past CSR initiatives, identify shortcomings, and build upon successful frameworks. Real- world examples, such as companies that have pivoted to greener practices and garnered public favour, highlight the potential benefits of aligning organisational values with those of Generation Alpha.

We also can't ignore the lessons learned from failures in communication strategies. The shift from traditional, top-down communication to more inclusive and interactive dialogue represents a significant change that businesses must embrace. Using past failures as learning points, companies can implement communication strategies that are more adaptive, inclusive, and engaging, addressing the unique needs and expectations of Generation Alpha.

In reality, preparing for uncertainty requires a broad-based approach. Agile methodologies that emphasise iterative learning, particularly from failures, can be invaluable. Planning for multiple scenarios, testing hypotheses, and being prepared to pivot quickly based on learnings can equip organisations to deal with the unknown. This proactive approach aligns well with the resilience and adaptability required to meet Generation Alpha's expectations.

Finally, the symbiotic relationship between innovation and learning from both failures and successes cannot be overstated. Businesses that encourage experimental thinking and are willing to make calculated risks will find themselves better prepared for the influx of Generation Alpha. This forward-thinking approach should ideally permeate every level of the organisation, fostering a pervasive culture of innovation and continuous improvement.

In conclusion, learning from both successes and failures offers the dual benefit of refining what works while recognising and mitigating potential pitfalls. Doing so equips organisations with practical strategies and the right mindset to embrace Generation Alpha. These lessons form an indispensable guide as we step into the future, aiming to create workplaces characterised by innovation, flexibility, and sustainability.

Chapter 11:
The Global Workforce

As we step into a world that grows increasingly interconnected, managing a global workforce effectively is now more crucial than ever. Harnessing the strengths of cross-cultural teams not only opens doors to diverse perspectives but also drives competitive edge and innovation. Leaders must cultivate an environment where cultural nuances are understood and appreciated, enabling smoother communication and collaboration. When operating across different time zones and geographies, challenges such as logistical hurdles and trust-building in remote settings come into play. Yet, with the right strategies, these can be transformed into opportunities for growth and efficiency. By leveraging international talents, companies can tap into unique skill sets and vibrant work ethics, fostering a more inclusive and dynamic workplace. Embracing this complexity and adapting to its demands doesn't just prepare us for future disruptions—it positions us to thrive in a landscape where the only constant is change.

Managing Cross-Cultural Teams

Leading a cross-cultural team isn't just about bridging geographical gaps; it's about leveraging diverse perspectives to drive innovation and problem-solving in the global workforce. As we look to integrate Generation Alpha, known for their inclusivity and digital savviness, the ability to navigate cultural differences becomes even more pivotal. Encouraging open communication and cultural awareness enables team members to share unique insights while fostering mutual respect. This involves understanding and valuing different communication styles, work habits, and viewpoints. By creating an environment that embraces diversity, leaders can tap into a broader range of ideas and solutions, ultimately enhancing team performance and cohesion. As a forward-thinking leader or HR professional, ensuring your cross-cultural team feels valued and understood is not just a courtesy; it's a strategic advantage that can propel your organisation towards sustainable success in a dynamically changing world.

Effective Communication and Understanding Cultural Nuances in a globalised work environment are indispensable for fostering collaboration and harnessing the diverse strengths of a cross-cultural team. As leaders, HR professionals, and strategists, honing these skills is paramount for successfully integrating Generation Alpha into our workplaces, environments inherently rich in cultural diversity.

Our understanding of effective communication must evolve alongside the work dynamics that Generation Alpha will bring. Given their distinct technological edge and diverse backgrounds, traditional communication strategies may not suffice. The first step is acknowledging the myriad facets of verbal and non-verbal communication, from the nuanced body language cues to the implicit meanings behind digital interactions.

Cultural nuances often manifest in subtle ways, impacting communication styles, workplace behaviours, and expectations. For instance, what is considered direct and straightforward in one culture might be perceived as rude or blunt in another. This delicate balance of respect and clarity is crucial when managing a multicultural team.

To foster effective communication, organisations must cultivate an environment where cultural intelligence is highly valued. It is about moving beyond mere tolerance of different cultures to the active promotion of cultural learning and empathy. This begins with leadership. Leaders must exemplify an inclusive mindset that seeks to understand and celebrate the diverse backgrounds within their teams.

The digital landscape further amplifies the challenge, as remote work becomes more prevalent. Generation Alpha, being digital natives, are adept in using technology for communication and collaboration. However, we must recognise that digital communication lacks the richness of face-to-face interactions. Without the benefit of physical presence, nuances can often be lost or misinterpreted. Thus, leaders must be adept at navigating these waters, ensuring clarity and mutual understanding regardless of the medium.

One effective approach is to encourage open channels of communication where team members feel safe to express their thoughts and concerns. Regular virtual meetings, forums, and feed-back sessions can help bridge gaps. However, it's also important to be aware of "communication fatigue" – the relentless barrage of emails, messages, and meetings can overwhelm team members, leading to disengagement.

Moreover, the importance of active listening cannot be overstated. In a culturally diverse team, active listening goes beyond hearing words – it involves understanding the context, emotions, and underlying sentiments. This practice fosters a deeper level of empathy and helps in addressing issues before they escalate into misunderstandings or conflicts.

Training sessions focused on cross-cultural communication and conflict resolution can be immensely beneficial. These programs should not be viewed as a tick-box exercise but as a continuous commitment to personal and professional development. By providing these resources, organisations demonstrate their dedication to creating a harmonious and productive workplace.

Equally important is the expression of gratitude and recognition. The manner in which appreciation is communicated can vary significantly across cultures. Understanding these differences ensures that praise and acknowledgment are received in the spirit they are intended, fostering motivation and a sense of belonging.

Generation Alpha, with their intrinsic understanding of global connectivity, can be a catalyst in breaking cultural barriers. However, they will also require guidance and mentorship in navigating the subtleties of cross-cultural interactions. As more influences shape their professional personas, the symbiotic relationship between senior and junior members will be key to building a cohesive and culturally rich workforce.

Another critical aspect is the implementation of policies that reflect cultural sensitivity. For instance, recognising and celebrating diverse cultural holidays, offering flexible working arrangements to accommodate different time zones, and providing language support can significantly enhance inclusivity. These policies should be reviewed regularly to remain aligned with the evolving cultural dynamics within the team.

Moreover, leveraging technology to support cultural learning can be highly effective. Virtual team-building exercises, online cultural sensitivity courses, and even AI-driven tools that provide real-time feedback on possible cultural faux pas can equip teams with the necessary tools to navigate cultural complexities.

The role of storytelling in bridging cultural gaps should not be underestimated. Encouraging team members to share their stories and experiences can foster a deeper understanding of each other's backgrounds, thereby fostering mutual respect and collaboration. These stories can become a treasury of the team's collective identity, enriching the organisational culture.

Ultimately, effective communication and understanding cultural nuances is not just about achieving operational harmony. It's about unleashing the full potential of a diverse workforce. When team members feel understood, respected, and valued, they are more likely to be engaged, innovative, and committed to the organisation's success.

In conclusion, the journey of integrating Generation Alpha into our workplaces demands a sophisticated grasp of cultural nuances and a commitment to fostering effective communication. By embracing these principles, we lay the groundwork for a future where our diverse human capital thrives, driving forward a culture of inclusivity, innovation, and global collaboration.

Leveraging Global Talents for Competitive Advantage is not just about casting a wider net; it's about strategically integrating diverse skills and perspectives to thrive in the fast-evolving workplace that Generation Alpha will soon populate. The concept of a global workforce is no longer a distant ideal; it's a present reality that forward-thinking leaders and HR professionals need to harness effectively. The aim is simple yet profound: leveraging global talents to create a dynamic, innovative, and competitive edge in the marketplace.

To begin with, the geographical boundaries that once limited the talent pool are now virtually non-existent, thanks to advancements in technology. This means organisations have the unprecedented opportunity to access a diverse array of skills and perspectives from every corner of the globe. When managed effectively, this diversity can lead to increased innovation, problem-solving capabilities, and operational resilience. In this context, Generation Alpha, with their inherent technological skills and global outlook, will be the torchbearers who can seamlessly navigate and invigorate this multicultural landscape.

It's essential to understand that leveraging global talent is not just about filling positions but about creating a culture of inclusivity and collaboration. Diversity in terms of nationality, cultural background, and life experiences can fuel creativity and lead to richer brainstorming sessions. Companies that can foster such environments are likely to see breakthroughs that more homogenous teams might miss. This brings us to the question: how can organisations structure themselves to fully exploit these advantages?

Firstly, organisations must prioritise building cross-cultural competence among their leaders and employees. This involves not only understanding but also genuinely appreciating the different cultural contexts from which their global talents originate. Training progr- ammes focused on cultural intelligence, language skills, and communication nuances could prove invaluable. This isn't about forcing everyone to fit into a single mould, but rather recognising and celebrating differences while finding common ground.

Generation Alpha is poised to be the most technologically savvy cohort to date, with a natural inclination for using digital tools to connect and collaborate. This offers a unique opportunity for businesses to implement advanced technologies such as AI, virtual reality, and collaborative platforms to bridge the physical gaps between geographically dispersed teams. Leveraging these technologies effectively can transform potential logistical challenges into strategic advantages, creating a truly interconnected global workforce.

The role of leadership cannot be overstated in this context. Leaders need to embody and promote a global mindset, demonstrating adaptability and empathy in their management styles. They should encourage input from all corners of their diverse teams and make it clear that every voice matters. Inclusive leadership practices are critical in ensuring that all team members feel valued and engaged, which in turn drives innovation and productivity.

Moreover, an organisation's ability to harness global talents hinges significantly on its flexibility and adaptability. This includes adapting

HR practices to be more inclusive of international candidates, providing remote work options, and ensuring that policies are equitable and culturally sensitive. Flexibility in working hours can help accommodate different time zones, while equitable compensation structures can make a global workforce feel fairly treated and motivated.

Beyond internal policies and practices, partnerships with educational institutions, both local and international, can be a powerful strategy for talent acquisition and development. Engaging with universities and training centres around the globe can help organisations tap into emerging talent pools early. Apprenticeships, internships, and exchange programmes can serve as effective bridges, providing a pathway for young, talented individuals from diverse backgrounds to integrate into the workforce seamlessly.

An effective way to leverage global talents is through collaborative projects that bring together employees from various parts of the world to solve complex problems. Such initiatives can be instrumental in fostering a spirit of global collaboration and innovation. Exposure to multiple viewpoints and problem-solving techniques can lead to more robust and creative solutions. Moreover, these projects can serve as learning opportunities, helping employees develop skills such as global project management, remote collaboration, and cross-cultural communication.

It's also important to address potential challenges head-on, such as language barriers and different work ethics. Investing in language training and creating a culture of open communication can mitigate some of these challenges. Similarly, aligning on common goals, establishing clear expectations, and fostering mutual respect can help bridge differences in work habits and attitudes, making collaboration more effective.

Lastly, a significant yet often overlooked aspect of leveraging global talent is recognising the importance of wellness and work-life balance. Organisations must ensure that their remote and international employees have access to resources and support systems that promote their well-being, recognizing that overworking or different cultural attitudes towards work can negatively impact productivity and morale. Flexible schedules and wellness programmes that are inclusive of all employees, irrespective of their location, can go a long way in showing that the organisation values their contribution and cares for their overall well-being.

By turning these principles into action, companies can not only tap into a broader talent pool but also create a more innovative, agile, and competitive organisation. Generation Alpha, with their digital fluency and global perspective, will naturally thrive in such environments, pushing the boundaries of what's possible and driving the organisation forward.

It's clear that the future belongs to those who can successfully blend local expertise with global perspectives. Hence, turning the diversity of Generation Alpha into a competitive advantage requires a commitment to cultural competence, adaptive leadership, and the strategic use of technology. It's about building a workplace where every individual, irrespective of their background, can contribute their unique strengths and ideas.

The efforts to harness global talent for competitive advantage can transform organisations in profound ways, promoting inclusivity, innovation, and sustainable growth. As we prepare to welcome Generation Alpha into the workplace, let's make sure we're ready to embrace the richness they bring, leveraging their skills and perspectives to build a future that's not just competitive, but also equitable and inspiring.

In conclusion, the journey towards leveraging global talents for competitive advantage begins with an unwavering commitment to inclusivity and strategic innovation. It's a journey that requires patience, adaptability, and a deep appreciation for the diverse tapestry of human talent. Through thoughtful planning and execution, organisations can turn this vision into reality, setting the stage for a future where the global workforce, empowered by Generation Alpha, leads to unprecedented levels of success and innovation.

Remote Work and International Opportunities

As the world becomes more interconnected, the potential for remote work and international opportunities has never been greater. Generation Alpha, with its inherent tech-savviness and global mindset, will drive the demand for a workspace that isn't confined by geographical boundaries. This shift towards remote work not only opens doors for tapping into a diverse pool of talents from across the globe, but also challenges organisations to rethink how they manage and support distributed teams. The flexibility of remote work comes with its own set of logistical challenges, such as coordinating across time zones and fostering a sense of cohesion among team members who may never meet face-to-face. Yet, as we embrace these opportunities, building a robust framework for communication, trust, and accountability becomes crucial. By leveraging digital tools and fostering a culture of inclusivity and collaboration, leaders can overcome these barriers and create a truly global workforce where innovation and creativity flourish.

Overcoming Time Zone and Logistical Challenges might seem like a daunting task, but it's an essential aspect of harnessing the full potential of a global workforce. For forward-thinking leaders, HR professionals, and strategists, navigating these challenges calls for an innovative and flexible approach. Embracing diverse, geographically dispersed teams is not just a logistical necessity but a strategic advantage.

Firstly, let's consider the implications of time zones. Traditional 9-to-5 schedules no longer apply when team members are scattered across continents. Leaders must cultivate a culture where asynchronous communication becomes the norm. Tools like Slack, Microsoft Teams, and Trello can facilitate this, allowing team members to contribute at different times while keeping everyone in the loop.

Additionally, it is essential to establish clear and effective communication guidelines. Asynchronous interactions require clarity and precision to prevent misunderstandings. Encouraging brief but comprehensive updates can significantly reduce the noise and ensure everyone is on the same page. Setting expectations for response times can help manage workload and avoid any potential burnout.

But technology alone isn't enough. Generation Alpha, with their digital proficiency, can adapt quickly, but they also seek meaningful connections. Leaders should schedule regular check-ins and virtual face-to-face meetings. These interactions build rapport and foster a sense of belonging, mitigating the isolation that remote work can sometimes cause.

Moreover, it's crucial to acknowledge the cultural nuances within a global workforce. A one-size-fits-all approach to management won't suffice. Leaders must invest time in understanding cultural differences and how they affect communication styles, decision-making processes, and work ethics. This understanding can turn potential conflicts into opportunities for richer collaboration.

Addressing logistical challenges requires more than just managing time zones; it involves rethinking work processes. Flexibility should extend to deadlines and workload distribution. Consider using global workforce planning software to dynamically assign tasks based on both availability and expertise, thus optimising productivity across all regions.

In terms of scheduling meetings, finding a universally suitable time slot can be nearly impossible. Rotating meeting times can share the burden of inconvenience among all team members. It's also worth considering that not every meeting needs to be synchronous. Recording meetings for those who can't attend and sharing detailed minutes can ensure everyone stays informed.

Accessibility is another key factor. Ensure that all employees have access to the necessary tools and resources, regardless of their location. This might involve providing hardware, software, or even workspace stipends. It's about creating an equitable environment where geographical location doesn't inhibit someone's ability to contribute effectively.

On the logistical front, consider the administrative and legal aspects of employing a global workforce. Each country has its own employment laws, tax regulations, and compliance requirements. Partnering with global employment organisations or using specialised HR software can streamline these processes, reducing legal risks and administrative burdens.

Moreover, fostering a transparent work environment can enhance trust and accountability. Utilizing project management tools that offer visibility across all tasks and milestones keeps everyone aligned. Generation Alpha values transparency and purpose in their work; aligning on shared goals and tracking progress openly resonates with their ethos.

Time zones can also present challenges for collaboration on time-sensitive projects. Implementing a 'follow-the-sun' model, where work is handed off to colleagues in different time zones, can ensure continuous progress. This model requires meticulous planning and communication but can significantly enhance efficiency.

Encouraging local leadership can bridge the gap of distance and time. Appointing regional leaders who understand local contexts and can make swift decisions helps maintain agility. These leaders can act as liaisons, ensuring that centralised objectives align with regional execution.

Finally, nurturing a sense of collective identity within a dispersed team is vital. Company-wide virtual events, inclusive recognition programs, and transparent communication from leadership can foster a unified culture. Generation Alpha thrives in environments where they feel connected and integral to the company's mission.

Integrating Generation Alpha into a global workforce isn't without challenges, but the benefits far surpass the hurdles. By leveraging innovative strategies to overcome time zone and logistical challenges, organisations can unlock immense potential for innovation, flexibility, and sustainability. This approach not only prepares companies for the future but positions them as leaders in an increasingly interconnected world.

Building Trust and Accountability in Remote Teams has become a pivotal challenge in the new world of work. With Generation Alpha on the horizon, understanding how to effectively manage and inspire remote teams is more critical than ever. This generation, born into a world of digital saturation, has unique expectations and needs regarding work environments and managerial approaches. Here, we delve into strategies and principles to help leaders build a trustworthy and accountable remote team dynamic.

First, let's acknowledge that a foundation of trust is paramount. Without trust, no amount of accountability measures or technological tools can create a cohesive, productive team. For Generation Alpha, trust isn't just about reliability; it's deeply tied to transparency and authenticity. This generation has grown up scrutinising brands and institutions, demanding honesty and openness. As a leader, showing vulnerability, sharing challenges, and being transparent about decision-making processes can go a long way in building trust.

An effective way to foster trust is through consistent and open communication. Regular check-ins, be it weekly meetings or daily updates, help keep everyone on the same page. But communication shouldn't be one-dimensional. Encourage feedback loops where team members feel safe to voice concerns, provide suggestions, and share their insights without fear of retribution. This encourages a culture of mutual respect and understanding, key for building trust and accountability.

Establishing clear expectations is also critical. Each team member should have a well-defined role, with clear deliverables and timelines. Use collaborative tools to maintain visibility on tasks and progress. This not only helps in tracking productivity but also ensures everyone knows who is doing what, fostering a sense of reliability and trust.

A fundamental aspect of accountability is ownership. When team members feel a sense of ownership over their tasks and projects, they are more likely to follow through. Delegation should come with empowerment; provide the necessary resources and trust your team to execute their responsibilities. This empowers the individual and builds a culture where accountability is a shared value, not imposed from the top down.

Remote work often lacks the spontaneous interactions and informal exchanges that naturally build relationships and trust in a physical office. To compensate, create virtual social spaces where informal conversations can happen. Virtual coffee breaks, team-building online games, or social platforms dedicated to non-work-related discussions can facilitate bonding and reinforce trust among team members.

Measuring and celebrating achievements are equally important. Recognise and reward efforts, both big and small. This isn't just about financial incentives; public recognition, personal acknowledgements, and team-wide celebrations of milestones can significantly enhance motivation and accountability. When team members see their efforts appreciated, they are more likely to stay committed and accountable.

Conflict resolution is a facet of remote team management that demands attention. Address conflicts head-on and promptly. Create a safe and transparent process for conflict resolution, ensuring that everyone feels heard and respected. This helps maintain an environment of trust and ensures that accountability doesn't falter in the face of disagreements.

The role of technology in supporting trust and accountability in remote teams can't be overstated. Employ tools that enhance visibility, communication, and collaboration. Project management software, communication platforms, and time-tracking tools can provide the infrastructure needed for a transparent and accountable remote work environment. However, it's crucial to balance supervision with autonomy; over-surveillance can erode trust.

Leadership plays a pivotal role. As a leader, modelling the behaviour you expect from your team is essential. Show up on time for virtual meetings, meet your deadlines, and engage actively in team discussions. Your actions set the tone for the team's culture and expectations regarding trust and accountability.

Cultural sensitivity is another layer to consider, especially in global remote teams. Understanding cultural nuances and respecting diversity can aid in creating a cohesive team where trust and accountability thrive. Encourage openness about cultural differences and provide platforms for team members to learn about and appreciate each other's backgrounds.

Training and development should not take a back seat in remote settings. Invest in upskilling and continuous education for your team. Online courses, virtual workshops, and mentorship programs can ensure that your team remains competent, boosting their confidence and accountability in their roles. This is particularly vital for Generation Alpha, who value growth and learning opportunities.

Trust and accountability are also deeply tied to mental and emotional well-being. Ensure that your team feels supported, especially during challenging times. Provide resources for mental health, create flexible working arrangements, and foster an environment where asking for help is not stigmatised. A team that feels cared for will naturally be more trustworthy and accountable.

Innovation in remote work practices can also enhance trust and accountability. Experiment with new approaches and be open to feedback. Whether it's changing the meeting structures, trialling new collaborative tools, or redefining work hours, stay adaptable. Showing that you're willing to evolve and prioritise the team's needs will strengthen trust.

Finally, remember that building trust and accountability in remote teams is an ongoing process. It requires continuous effort, reflection, and adaptation. Stay engaged with your team, seek regular feedback, and be prepared to make necessary adjustments. With Generation Alpha entering the workforce, these principles will not only help you manage remote teams effectively but also create an environment where this new generation can thrive, innovate, and drive your organisation forward.

Chapter 12:
Corporate Social Responsibility (CSR)

Corporate Social Responsibility (CSR) has transcended from being a mere buzzword to a pivotal aspect of corporate strategy, particularly as Generation Alpha transitions into the workplace. This generation, characterised by their digital prowess and inherent environmental consciousness, demands more than traditional business practices. They expect corporations to hold a mirror to their values by prioritising sustainable practices, ethical behaviour, and social equity. The intertwining of ESG principles (Environmental, Social, and Governance) with corporate objectives isn't just good ethics; it's good business. Companies that align their CSR initiatives with the core values of Generation Alpha will not only enhance their brand reputation but also foster loyalty and drive innovation. This synergy between CSR and Generation Alpha sets a foundation for a future where business growth and societal good go hand in hand, creating a more engaged, productive, and innovative workforce.

Aligning Values: CSR and Generation Alpha

Aligning corporate social responsibility (CSR) with the values of Generation Alpha isn't just a strategic move—it's essential for future-proofing your organisation. Generation Alpha, with their innate digital fluency and heightened ethical consciousness, expect more from businesses than just quality products or services. They prioritise environmental sustainability and social impact, demanding transparency and accountability. Integrating these values into your CSR initiatives will not only resonate with this emerging generation but also foster a culture of integrity and purpose within your organisation. By authentically embedding these principles into your corporate DNA, you'll not only attract and retain the best talent but also cultivate a loyal consumer base that believes in your mission. Inspiring and motivating your team through meaningful CSR efforts will lead to groundbreaking innovations that make a real difference—ensuring that your company thrives in a rapidly changing world.

Environmental Sustainability is not merely a buzzword for Generation Alpha; it is a way of life. This young generation is growing up with a heightened awareness of the environmental challenges facing the planet and a deep-seated commitment to address them. For forward-thinking leaders and HR professionals, understanding this intrinsic value is vital in fostering a workplace conducive to their values and innovative potential.

Environmental sustainability in the workplace goes beyond just reducing paper usage or implementing recycling programmes. To truly resonate with Generation Alpha, businesses need to embed sustainable practices into the organisational DNA. This means rethinking everything from office design and energy consumption to the very products and services offered.

This transformation isn't just about ticking boxes for corporate social responsibility (CSR) reports. Incorporating sustainable practices has tangible benefits including cost savings, improved brand reputation, and increased employee engagement. When companies commit to authentic, consistent sustainability efforts, they create a culture that Generation Alpha will both respect and want to be a part of.

One of the initial steps towards achieving this is by redesigning workspaces to be more eco-friendly. Offices can be refurbished using sustainable materials, and energy-efficient appliances can replace older systems. Simple changes like better insulation and smart thermostats can significantly reduce energy consumption. Moreover, fostering a culture where employees are encouraged to switch off lights and devices when not in use reinforces the importance of these small, everyday actions.

Then there's the idea of creating green spaces within the office environment. It's no secret that a connection to nature improves one's well-being, productivity, and creativity. Indoor plants, rooftop gardens, or even dedicated green zones where employees can relax can make a significant difference. These green spaces are not just décorative; they are integral to a holistic approach to sustainability and provide tangible health benefits.

Energy use is perhaps one of the most impactful areas. Transitioning to renewable energy sources like solar or wind is no longer a far-fetched ideal; it's a practical and responsible choice. Companies can also adopt energy management systems that monitor and optimise energy usage in real-time. Generation Alpha wants to see this kind of commitment; they're looking for employers who are making sincere efforts to reduce their carbon footprint.

We also need to consider the materials and resources utilised in the workplace. Choosing sustainable and ethical suppliers shows a commitment that transcends the immediate office environment. Whether it's the paper used in printers or the coffee in the breakroom, these choices reflect an organisation's broader ethos. By aligning purchasing decisions with sustainable practices, companies send a clear message about their values.

Environmental sustainability also involves minimising waste. A zero-waste goal might seem ambitious, but many companies are taking substantial steps in this direction by eliminating single-use plastics and maximising recycling efforts. Practices such as composting organic waste and implementing rigorous recycling programmes can significantly reduce an organisation's environmental impact.

To truly embed environmental sustainability into the workplace culture, education and engagement are crucial. Regular workshops, training sessions, and sustainability initiatives can help keep the workforce informed and motivated. Generation Alpha, in particular, will appreciate being part of a company that educates and empowers its employees to make environmentally friendly choices both at work and in their personal lives.

Technology plays a pivotal role in achieving these sustainability goals. Smart building systems that monitor climate control, lighting, and water usage can optimise efficiency and reduce waste. Digital platforms can also facilitate remote work, thus minimising the carbon footprint associated with commuting. These technological solutions not only improve sustainability but also resonate with Generation Alpha's affinity for digital innovation.

Moreover, businesses should aim for transparency in their sustainability efforts. Generation Alpha values honesty and will scrutinise companies that engage in greenwashing. It's essential to communicate goals, progress, and setbacks openly. Regular reporting and third-party audits can enhance credibility and demonstrate a genuine commitment to environmental sustainability.

Collaboration extends beyond the office walls. Partnering with other companies, local governments, and non-profits can amplify efforts and create a broader impact. These alliances can result in community projects, joint ventures in green technologies, and shared commitments to sustainable development goals. Such collaborative efforts not only enhance sustainability but also strengthen the company's standing within the community.

As leaders and HR professionals, it's imperative to keep an eye on future trends and innovations in sustainability. Whether it's new materials, cutting-edge energy solutions, or innovative waste management systems, staying ahead of the curve will demonstrate to Generation Alpha that the company is forward-thinking and committed to continuous improvement.

In conclusion, embracing environmental sustainability is not just the right thing to do; it's a strategic necessity. For Generation Alpha, it's about seeing tangible, authentic actions aligned with their core values. By integrating sustainable practices into every aspect of the workplace, companies do more than attract and retain top talent; they inspire a movement towards a more sustainable and innovative future.

Social Impact and Community Engagement are not just buzzwords in the lexicon of modern business practices; they are crucial pillars in fostering a workplace that resonates with the values of Generation Alpha. As leaders striving to integrate this next generation into our work environments, we must understand their intrinsic motivations for social awareness and active engagement within their communities.

For Generation Alpha, social responsibility isn't optional; it's embedded in their DNA. They've grown up in an era where movements and causes are not just watched from the sidelines but actively participated in through the power of social media and digital platforms. If we want to attract and retain these future leaders, our organisations must reflect a deep commitment to social impact, both locally and globally.

Community engagement isn't simply about charity drives or financial contributions. It's about creating pathways where Generation Alpha can see the tangible impact of their efforts. One strategy is to initiate programmes where employees can take paid time off to volunteer in community projects. This not only benefits the community but also allows employees to bond over shared values, thereby enhancing workplace culture.

In fostering a genuine sense of social impact, consider the integration of sustainable business practices into your operations. Generation Alpha is particularly attentive to environmental issues, having been educated on climate change from a young age. Initiatives like reducing carbon footprints, promoting recycling within the office, and supporting green technologies can go a long way in aligning with their values.

Moreover, our approach to community engagement must be holistic. It's not enough to focus solely on environmental sustainability; we must also address issues of social equity and inclusion. This means not just supporting external community initiatives but also creating an inclusive workspace where everyone feels valued and empowered to contribute.

One innovative approach is to establish partnerships with local organisations and NGOs, providing avenues for employees to participate in community outreach programmes. These partnerships should be mutually beneficial, allowing employees to utilise their skills for community betterment while also gaining valuable experiences that enhance their professional development.

Another important aspect is transparency. Generation Alpha values openness and honesty, and they expect this from their employers. Regularly communicating the impacts of your social responsibility initiatives, both successes and areas for improvement, fosters a sense of trust and shared purpose. Publishing annual CSR reports and maintaining an open dialogue through town halls or internal newsletters can achieve this effectively.

Our roles as future-centric leaders extend beyond balancing the books or driving innovation; we must also be stewards of social impact.

Take the lead in promoting initiatives that resonate with Generation Alpha's innate desire for social justice and environmental sustainability. By doing so, we transform workplaces into hubs of community and civic engagement.

A practical step is to develop an internal committee dedicated to social impact projects, comprising members across different levels and departments. This committee can spearhead various initiatives, from organising community clean-up days to championing diversity forums. It's about decentralising the responsibility and empowering every employee to take ownership of these efforts.

Let's also not overlook the role of education in driving social impact. Organise workshops and training sessions focusing on sustainable practices, inclusive behaviors, and community service. Equip your employees, especially those from Generation Alpha, with the knowledge and skills to make informed and impactful contributions both within and outside the workplace.

Community engagement can also be furthered through leveraging technology. Create digital platforms or apps that track and reward community service efforts. Gamify these initiatives to make them more engaging and rewarding. Generation Alpha, being digital natives, would find such platforms intuitive and motivating.

It's worth noting that social impact and community engagement cannot be seen as separate from the core business strategy. Align these initiatives with your company's mission and values. This alignment makes the efforts genuine and ensures that they are sustainable in the long run, rather than being just another box-ticking exercise.

In summary, integrating Generation Alpha into the workplace isn't merely about adapting to their technological proficiencies or rethinking physical workspaces. It's about creating a culture where social responsibility and community engagement are at the forefront.

Leadership teams that embrace this holistic approach will find themselves not only more attractive to top talent from this generation but also positioned as forward-thinking and socially conscious organisations in the global marketplace.

As we engage Generation Alpha in meaningful ways, let's remember that our actions today shape the leaders of tomorrow. By fostering a work environment that prioritises social impact and community engagement, we're not just preparing for the future; we're actively moulding it.

Measuring Impact: Beyond Profits

In the evolving landscape of Corporate Social Responsibility (CSR), the significance of measuring impact extends far beyond mere financial gains. Forward-thinking leaders and HR professionals must recognise that Generation Alpha, with their intrinsic values of sustainability and social responsibility, will demand a more holistic approach to assessing corporate success. This means evaluating environmental stewardship, societal contributions, and ethical governance as critical metrics. By adopting comprehensive impact measurement strategies, organisations demonstrate their genuine commitment to making a difference, cultivating trust and loyalty both within their workforce and among consumers. Ultimately, it's not just about the bottom line; it's about integrating purpose with profit to foster enduring, positive change.

Transparency in CSR Efforts is not just a buzzword; it's becoming a cornerstone for businesses serious about adapting to the sensibilities of Generation Alpha. This generation, steeped in digital awareness and eco-consciousness from a young age, values authenticity and openness in corporate actions. Transparency in CSR isn't merely a moral imperative but also a strategic necessity for fostering trust, loyalty, and long-term engagement with both employees and consumers.

Generation Alpha, having grown up amidst an ever-expanding digital landscape, has an unparalleled ability to access, share, and scrutinise information. This unique characteristic means they will demand transparency not just in how companies talk about their social responsibility initiatives but also in how they execute them. Organisations, therefore, must be prepared to present clear, verifiable, and accessible data on their CSR efforts.

Transparency in CSR efforts calls for detailed reporting. Gone are the days when a glossy annual report would suffice. Today, ongoing, granular updates via multiple channels – think social media, dedicated microsites, and interactive dashboards – are vital. Real-time tracking of initiatives like carbon footprint reduction or charitable contributions helps maintain credibility.

It's essential to adopt inclusive metrics that go beyond mere financial impacts. Sure, profits matter, but Generation Alpha will want to see the broader societal and environmental benefits of corporate initiatives. By adopting frameworks such as the Global Reporting Initiative (GRI) or the United Nations Sustainable Development Goals (SDGs), companies can provide a robust, multifaceted view of their CSR performance.

Integral to transparency is stakeholder engagement. It is not a one-way communication channel; it's a dialogue. Actively involving employees, customers, and communities in CSR planning and execution ensures that initiatives are grounded in genuine needs and interests. Regular stakeholder feedback loops can refine and optimise ongoing projects, providing an additional layer of transparency.

External validation also plays a crucial role. Third-party audits, certifications, and recognitions from reputable bodies lend credibility and ultimately build public trust. Companies should seek to get their CSR reports audited by independent agencies, which helps in holding them accountable and verifying their claims.

Social media is an invaluable tool in the transparency toolkit. Companies should leverage these platforms not only to broadcast their CSR successes but also to candidly discuss challenges and setbacks. Posts, stories, and live Q&A sessions can personalise corporate narratives, making the company seem more relatable and committed to honest practices.

Transparency extends internally as well. Open communication with employees about CSR goals and progress can foster a culture of shared responsibility and pride. This can be achieved through internal newsletters, town hall meetings, and even integrating CSR modules into ongoing training programs. Clear communication around why certain initiatives are chosen and how they align with corporate values can significantly enhance employee buy-in.

Harnessing technology to drive Transparency in CSR Efforts may entail blockchain applications for enhanced traceability and verification. For instance, supply chain transparency can be significantly improved, providing unalterable records of sustainable sourcing practices. Such technologies will resonate deeply with the tech-savvy Generation Alpha.

Real transparency means not shying away from the complexities and imperfections of the journey. Highlighting both successes and areas needing improvement can build a narrative of continuous growth and sincere effort. This openness can paradoxically build more trust than polished, overly positive reports, as it demonstrates a genuine commitment to progress.

Transparency in CSR also involves financial transparency. Disclosing how much of a company's budget is allocated to various CSR initiatives and the economic impact of these investments can offer a comprehensive view of the organisation's priorities. Financial transparency helps stakeholders see the tangible commitment the company has made towards its CSR goals.

Moreover, transparency fosters accountability. Publicly shared CSR goals and deadlines mean companies can be held accountable by a much broader audience. This not only includes investors who are increasingly concerned with ESG (Environmental, Social, Governance) metrics but also the community and consumers who can exert pressure for better practices if needed.

Transparency in CSR efforts is not without its challenges. There is always a risk of information being misinterpreted or the demand for data becoming overwhelming. However, the potential benefits in terms of strengthened relationships, increased trust, and enhanced corporate reputation far outweigh these challenges. Thus, having a clear strategy for data management and communication is vital.

Legal considerations also come into play. Ensuring that CSR disclosures comply with regulations and are not misleading is critical. Working with legal teams to navigate these waters ensures that transparency efforts support rather than compromise the company's position.

In sum, **transparency in CSR efforts** is indispensable for building a future-facing, trustworthy, and resilient organisation that aligns with the values of Generation Alpha. By embracing transparent practices, leaders and HR professionals can create a workplace culture that not only attracts but retains and inspires the next generation of talent. Doing so paves the way for a sustainable, equitable, and innovative future.

Long-Term Commitments and Sustainable Growth are not merely buzzwords in the context of integrating Generation Alpha into the workforce. They form the cornerstone of a resilient and forward-thinking enterprise. This generation, more than any before it, holds profound expectations for corporate responsibility and sustainable practices, making it imperative for organisations to align their long-term strategies accordingly.

In the pursuit of *sustainable growth*, companies need to reimagine their commitment to environmental and social responsibilities. Generation Alpha's affinity for sustainability isn't just a passing phase—it's a deeply ingrained value that will influence their career choices and loyalty to employers. For businesses to attract and retain top talent from this generation, a genuine and ongoing commitment to sustainability is non-negotiable.

Consider how innovation ties into sustainability. To meet the expectations of Generation Alpha, companies must innovate continuously—not just for the sake of growth but for the betterment of the environment and society. This goes beyond integrating eco-friendly practices; it involves rethinking entire business models to ensure long-term viability and positive societal impact.

Organisations are increasingly judged not just by their profits but by their societal contributions. Generation Alpha will scrutinise corporate actions, pushing businesses to demonstrate tangible results in their sustainability efforts. It's about making real change and not just greenwashing. This means adopting renewable energy, reducing waste, and ensuring ethical supply chains.

Achieving sustainable growth also involves redefining success metrics. Financial performance remains important, but it should now be complemented by metrics such as carbon footprint, social impact, and employee well-being. The integration of ESG (Environmental, Social, and Governance) criteria into corporate strategy will be critical for meeting Generation Alpha's expectations and for ensuring long-term success.

Companies aiming for sustainable growth must engage in **long-term partnerships** with stakeholders, including governments, NGOs, and local communities. Such collaborations can help businesses address complex sustainability challenges that they can't tackle alone. For Generation Alpha, seeing a company work alongside various stakeholders to generate positive environmental and social outcomes will be a significant differentiator.

Incorporating sustainability into the workplace culture is another pivotal aspect. Employees at all levels should understand and feel connected to the company's sustainability goals. This can be achieved through regular training, transparent communication, and integrating sustainability into everyday workflows. Creating a culture where every employee feels they can contribute to the company's long-term commitments will resonate well with the values of Generation Alpha.

Leadership plays a crucial role in advancing long-term commitments and sustainability. Leaders must walk the talk, embodying the principles of sustainable growth in their actions and decisions. They should inspire and motivate their teams to pursue sustainability goals passionately and diligently. By setting an example, leaders can galvanise the entire organisation to move toward a more sustainable future.

Moreover, fostering a flexible and innovative mindset within the organisation is essential. The dynamic nature of sustainability challenges requires businesses to be agile and adaptable. Encouraging risk-taking, experimenting with new ideas, and learning from failures will be key to finding effective and sustainable solutions. Generation Alpha, with its openness to experimentation and innovation, will thrive in such environments.

Technology will be a significant enabler of sustainable growth. Leveraging cutting-edge technologies like artificial intelligence, blockchain, and the Internet of Things can help businesses streamline operations, reduce environmental impact, and increase transparency. By investing in technology, companies can develop sustainable solutions that address the needs of the present without compromising the future.

Sustainable growth isn't solely about environmental stewardship; it also encompasses social equity. Ensuring fair labour practices, promoting diversity, equity, and inclusion (DEI), and positively impacting local communities are all essential aspects. Generation Alpha expects employers to be champions of social justice and equity, making it critical for companies to embed these principles into their core practices.

Financial resilience is another facet of sustainable growth. By adopting long-term sustainability strategies, companies can mitigate risks associated with resource scarcity, regulatory changes, and shifting consumer preferences. This approach makes businesses more robust and better prepared to navigate future uncertainties while continuing to grow and thrive.

The commitment to sustainability must permeate the entire value chain—from sourcing raw materials to delivering the final product. Companies need to scrutinise their suppliers, logistics, and manufacturing processes to ensure they align with sustainability goals. This may involve working with suppliers to implement sustainable practices or investing in cleaner technologies.

Engaging with consumers on sustainability issues creates a virtuous cycle of accountability and improvement. Transparent communication about sustainability initiatives and progress can build trust and loyalty among consumers. For Generation Alpha, whose purchasing decisions are heavily influenced by a company's values and actions, this can significantly enhance brand reputation and customer loyalty.

Furthermore, long-term commitments to sustainability can drive competitive advantage. Companies that lead in sustainability are often seen as innovators and industry leaders. This not only attracts talent but also opens up new market opportunities and strengthens the brand. By prioritising sustainability, businesses position themselves favourably in the eyes of consumers, investors, and prospective employees.

In conclusion, integrating Generation Alpha into the workplace goes hand in hand with committing to long-term sustainability and growth. It's about aligning organisational goals with the values of a generation that prioritises environmental and social responsibility. By embedding these principles into the core of their operations, companies can ensure lasting success and secure a thriving future for all.

Chapter 13:
The Consumer Influence

As we look ahead, Generation Alpha's dual roles as consumers and employees will significantly shape the work landscape. The businesses that align their strategies to meet the evolving expectations of this generation will gain a competitive edge. This cohort values authenticity and transparency more than their predecessors, seeking brands that genuinely reflect their own principles, particularly in areas like sustainability and social responsibility. As employees, they're likely to favour companies with ethical practices and meaningful social impact, which in turn would reinforce their brand loyalty as consumers. In essence, the lines between consumer preferences and employment choices will blur, driving organisations to integrate corporate social responsibility deeply into their business models. By fostering authenticity in every aspect of their operations, companies can resonate with Generation Alpha, not only attracting them but also retaining their trust and loyalty in a rapidly changing marketplace.

Generation Alpha as Consumers and Employees

Generation Alpha is poised to redefine the landscape as both consumers and employees, blending their tech-savvy nature with an unwavering commitment to social responsibility. Unlike any previous generation, they've been immersed in a digital universe from birth, making them not just digital adopters but digital natives. This brings an expectation for seamless, personalized experiences that brands must meet to gain their loyalty. As employees, they value flexibility, inclusivity, and innovation, shaping workplaces to be more adaptable and diverse. Companies that recognise and invest in these values will not only attract top talent but will also cultivate a workforce capable of driving continuous transformation. So, as we prepare for their influx into the professional world, it's imperative to align organisational goals with the unique characteristics and aspirations of Generation Alpha. Embracing their influence could be the key to thriving in tomorrow's marketplace.

The Impact on Brand Loyalty and Employment Choices offers a unique lens through which to examine the future of work, particularly as it intersects with Generation Alpha. This cohort, born into an era saturated with digital advancements and a heightened awareness of social responsibility, brings with it new expectations and demands that will reshuffle traditional business paradigms. If you're a forward-thinking leader or HR professional, understanding these shifts isn't just beneficial—it's essential.

You might ask, why should brand loyalty matter in the context of employment choices? To Generation Alpha, the two are inherently linked. For a generation that places enormous value on authenticity and transparency, a company's brand isn't just about the products or services it offers but also about its ethos, how it treats its employees, and its commitment to broader societal issues. These young talents will gauge a company's worthiness to join based on its brand integrity before they ever step foot in an interview room.

In today's competitive landscape, traditional perks like salaries and bonuses simply won't cut it. The brand's reputation, its stance on sustainability, and its social impact will play pivotal roles in attracting and retaining top talent from Generation Alpha. This shift necessitates a rebranding exercise for many organisations, focusing not just on customer acquisition but on employee satisfaction as well.

Take, for instance, the importance of sustainability. Generation Alpha demands that companies adopt eco-friendly practices and contribute to environmental conservation. When they're considering which employer to choose, a firm's sustainability credentials can be a decisive factor. Companies that fail to meet these expectations might find themselves struggling to attract this new wave of conscientious employees.

The influence of social responsibility extends beyond environmental concerns. Generation Alpha expects employers to take stands on human rights, diversity, and social justice. It's not enough to have these values enshrined in your mission statement; action is imperative. Organisations must continuously demonstrate their commitment to these causes through transparent reporting and real-world impact, lest they risk losing the loyalty of both consumers and potential employees.

Brand loyalty among Generation Alpha also involves a deeper level of engagement with technology. This cohort is a group of digital natives, so they will naturally gravitate towards companies that are tech-savvy and innovative. Businesses leveraging cutting-edge technologies, such as AI and blockchain, will not just attract customers but also capture the interest of prospective employees who want to be part of forward-thinking organisations.

The paradigm shift isn't restricted to job applicants' perspectives. Hiring processes and employment structures will need to adapt as well. With a strong preference for flexible work arrangements, Generation Alpha will be more inclined to choose companies that offer remote or hybrid work models. Traditional 9-to-5 jobs could soon be a relic of the past, making way for more personalised, adaptable work schedules.

But flexibility isn't just about where and when work happens; it's also about career pathways. Generation Alpha values continuous learning and skill development, which means companies need to provide an array of opportunities for professional growth.

Microlearning platforms, online courses, and flexible career ladders will be vital in retaining this dynamic workforce.

Brand loyalty and employment choices are also influenced by how businesses treat their current employees. Transparency in communication, robust mental health support, and a strong employee advocacy program will not only enhance retention but also make the brand more appealing to fresh talent. Young professionals want to work for companies that invest in their people.

Social media amplifies this effect exponentially. Brand loyalty can soar or plummet based on a single tweet or Instagram post. Generation Alpha follows brands closely on these platforms and can easily access stories from current employees about what it's like to work there. Organisations need to curate their online presence meticulously, ensuring their digital footprint reflects their core values and mission accurately.

The gig economy's rise also intertwines with brand loyalty and employment choices. Many within Generation Alpha will explore gig work before settling into longer-term roles. Their experiences as freelancers will shape their perceptions of potential full-time employers. Companies can attract these gig workers by offering short-term projects that align with their capabilities and interests, thereby building a pipeline of talent who may later seek permanent positions.

Moreover, companies who offer strong mentorship programs can enhance brand loyalty. Generation Alpha seeks guidance and values relationships with seasoned professionals who can provide insights and aid in career development. A robust mentorship culture often translates into increased employee satisfaction and retention, both crucial components of brand loyalty.

Alongside these points, it's crucial to mention the role of ethical marketing. Authentic engagement, coupled with a commitment to truth in advertising, can significantly affect Generation Alpha's perception of a brand. They are savvy consumers and prospective employees, quick to spot and reject inauthenticity or deceptive practices.

Finally, the geographical aspect plays a role too. As global citizens, Generation Alpha is more open to remote opportunities across borders. Companies leveraging this by promoting their inclusive and adaptive workplace cultures can attract top talent from anywhere in the world. These moves can build a strong, loyal brand community eager to innovate and drive the company forward.

In summary, as the landscape of brand loyalty evolves, companies must keep pace with it to remain compelling to Generation Alpha. It's not merely about adapting to new trends but embracing a holistic transformation in how businesses operate. Integrating sustainability, transparency, technological innovation, and flexible work environments can set organisations apart in this new era, spearheaded by Generation Alpha.

Pioneering leaders and HR professionals should start aligning their corporate strategies with the values and expectations that Generation Alpha holds dear. By doing so, they'll not only secure a loyal customer base but also a driven, committed workforce ready to conquer the future.

Authenticity and Transparency

In a workplace increasingly shaped by Generation Alpha's values, authenticity and transparency aren't just buzzwords—they're non-negotiables. As forward-thinking leaders and HR professionals, understanding that this generation demands brands and companies to walk the talk is paramount. Younger employees and consumers alike gravitate towards organisations that practice what they preach, whether it's in sustainability efforts or social responsibility. By committing to transparent practices, companies foster genuine trust and loyalty, which in turn drives innovation and long-term success. It isn't merely a strategy; it's a commitment to creating a workplace culture where ethical behaviour and straightforward communication are cornerstones, aligning with Generation Alpha's core expectations for the future. Ultimately, this dedication to honesty and openness differentiates thriving companies from those that will struggle to adapt in an evolving market influenced significantly by these new generational norms.

Building Brand Trust Through Genuine Engagement lies at the heart of establishing a meaningful connection with Generation Alpha. In an increasingly digital world, brands have a golden opportunity to build trust and loyalty through authentic interactions. This isn't just about transparent marketing; it involves creating genuine relationships that resonate on a deeper level. Generation Alpha, born into a tech-savvy era, has refined instincts for identifying authenticity. Their trust, once gained, can turn into powerful advocacy for your brand.

Start by understanding that Generation Alpha values actions over words. They're growing up in an era where information is at their fingertips, and they're quite adept at distinguishing between fact and fiction. Therefore, companies must go beyond flashy advertisements and bold claims. It's about demonstrating genuine commitment to values like sustainability, inclusivity, and social responsibility. This age group isn't just looking for a product or service; they want to align with brands that mirror their own principles and ethics.

Engagement with Generation Alpha through social media is pivotal. They are highly active on platforms like TikTok, Instagram, and emerging networks. To build trust, brands should focus on creating content that fosters an interactive community rather than a one-way street of information. For instance, user-generated content, where businesses encourage users to share their own experiences, can create a sense of belonging and authenticity. It transforms customers into brand ambassadors, furthering the trust loop.

Simplicity and transparency in communication are also critical. Overly complicated or long-winded messaging can alienate this generation. Instead, brands should look to communicate clearly, directly, and honestly. Whether it's about how products are sourced, the company's environmental impact, or the treatment of employees, being straightforward earns respect. This transparency applies to all facets—from marketing campaigns to customer service interactions.

Additionally, incorporating social proof is a powerful strategy. Testimonials, reviews, and case studies provide tangible evidence of a brand's reliability and effectiveness. When Generation Alpha sees people like themselves having positive experiences, their trust levels rise. However, it's essential to ensure these testimonials are genuine and not fabricated, as anything less can backfire spectacularly.

Interactive and immersive experiences are another intriguing pathway to engagement. Think augmented reality (AR) and virtual reality (VR) not just for entertainment, but as tools for customers to interact with products in a virtual space. For instance, trying on clothes virtually or experiencing a product's functionality in a three-dimensional realm can dramatically enhance trust. It allows potential customers to interact with the brand in an innovative, yet meaningful way.

Co-creation is a concept that invites the audience to participate in the development of products or services. Allowing Generation Alpha to take part in designing or customising aspects of their products can deepen their investment in the brand. This method not only builds trust but also fosters a sense of ownership and loyalty that is highly valuable.

Emphasising corporate social responsibility (CSR) efforts can also solidify trust. Generation Alpha is incredibly aware of societal issues and gravitates towards brands that take a firm and active role in making the world a better place. Be it through initiatives to reduce carbon footprints, supporting social justice causes, or contributing to community well-being, these actions speak volumes. Brands must ensure their CSR efforts are consistent and well-communicated to fully engage this ethically-minded generation.

However, it's vital to avoid the pitfalls of 'performative' CSR. Mere token gestures won't cut it for Generation Alpha. They crave substance and continuity. Longevity in CSR programs and genuine community involvement send a clear message that a brand's values are not merely seasonal or trendy. Integrating these efforts into the core business strategy demonstrates enduring commitment.

Personalisation in communication and service is another realm where brands can excel. Generation Alpha expects a more tailored experience. Utilising data analytics to understand their preferences and behaviours allows brands to offer personalised recommendations, content, and experiences. This tailored approach can significantly enhance trust, as it reflects an understanding and appreciation of the individual's interests.

Not to be overlooked is the role of ethical marketing practices. Avoiding manipulative tactics and instead focusing on truthfulness and customer well-being can differentiate a brand. Generation Alpha is likely to shun businesses employing deceitful or overly aggressive marketing techniques. Ethical marketing, characterised by clarity and respect for the consumer, fosters long-term trust.

Engagement extends to customer service as well. Brands must ensure they offer compassionate and responsive service across all touchpoints. Generation Alpha expects fast and effective resolutions to their inquiries and issues. Employing AI chatbots for initial interactions followed by seamless human support ensures a positive and trustworthy service experience.

Listening and responding to feedback is an essential element of genuine engagement. Invite feedback consistently and show you value it by implementing changes where possible. This not only builds trust but demonstrates a brand's commitment to continuous improvement and customer satisfaction.

Finally, advocating for transparency in supply chains is crucial. Generation Alpha cares about where and how products are made. Providing insights into the production process and ensuring ethical sourcing practices resonate deeply with this generation. Transparency here can mean the difference between a loyal customer and a sceptic.

In essence, building brand trust through genuine engagement isn't an isolated strategy but a comprehensive approach interwoven into every aspect of a brand's operations and ethos. By understanding and prioritising the values of Generation Alpha, brands can foster deep, sustained trust that transcends traditional customer-brand relationships.

Ethical Marketing and Social Responsibility are more than mere buzzwords in today's corporate lexicon. In the context of Generation Alpha, these concepts evolve into indispensable pillars that uphold the social contract between businesses and the communities they serve. This youngest generational cohort, born starting from 2010 onwards, has been raised in an era where awareness of social issues and digital connectivity are at their zenith. As they grow into future employees, leaders, and consumers, their behavioural tendencies and expectations will reshape how organisations approach ethical marketing and corporate social responsibility (CSR).

Businesses that wish to remain relevant and appealing to Generation Alpha must grasp the significance of ethical marketing.

This isn't just about avoiding deceit; it's about embodying transparency, honesty, and integrity in every interaction. For Generation Alpha, knowing that a brand is committed to these values can strongly influence their loyalty and trust. They value brands that are aligned with their social and environmental values—a trend already visible in their predecessors, Gen Z, but expected to intensify with the Alphas.

Incorporating social responsibility into your business model becomes more about everyday practice and less about grand gestures. Generation Alpha, exposed to an unprecedented flow of information from a young age, can quickly discern between superficial tokenism and genuine commitment. As a leader, marketer, or HR professional, your challenge is to weave social responsibility into the fabric of your company culture, ensuring that every act, no matter how small, echoes ethical principles.

Let's delve into specific strategies. Transparency in marketing involves clear, honest communication about your product's sourcing, manufacturing process, and environmental impact. It's not just about being truthful but also being open about your flaws and what you're doing to address them. Generation Alpha appreciates brands willing to share their journey candidly, including the challenges they face and the steps taken to overcome them. This sort of radical transparency can turn potential weaknesses into strengths.

Another critical aspect is participative marketing. This involves creating campaigns that invite Generation Alpha to be a part of the conversation, encouraging user-generated content, crowdsourcing ideas, and involving them in product development stages through feedback loops. This level of engagement fosters a sense of ownership and belonging, transforming them from passive consumers to active participants in your brand's story.

Moreover, ethical marketing for Generation Alpha is closely tied to sustainability. They heavily scrutinise the ecological impact of their consumption choices. Thus, promoting sustainability must go beyond mere marketing claims; it requires actual, demonstrable action. For instance, employing eco-friendly packaging, adopting carbon-neutral shipping practices, or donating a portion of profits to environmental causes can resonate deeply with Generation Alpha.

Social responsibility, on the other hand, extends the conversation into the impact your business has on society at large. This encompasses fair labour practices, community engagement, and initiatives that strive for social justice. Generation Alpha favours companies that champion equality and inclusivity, reflecting these values not only in their public communications but also in their internal practices. Employee diversity, equitable pay, and inclusive policies are non-negotiables in creating an appealing workspace for them.

Companies need a proactive stance towards issues like climate change, poverty alleviation, and digital inclusion. Being proactive rather than reactive means anticipating social needs and positioning your brand as a force for good before crises arise. It's about providing solutions and support in a manner that reflects genuine intent. Initiatives like community grants, volunteer programmes, and partnerships with NGOs can effectively convey your social responsibility commitment.

For the forward-thinking leader, integrating ethical marketing and social responsibility isn't merely an ethical requirement; it's a strategic imperative. Authenticity is key here—there's no room for hypocrisy. Any inconsistency between your words and actions is likely to be quickly spotted and heavily criticised by the tech-savvy Generation Alpha. Therefore, your marketing messages and corporate actions must align seamlessly.

One powerful tool at your disposal is social media. It's not just a platform for broadcasting but a medium for dialogue and feedback. Use it to showcase your CSR initiatives, provide real-time updates, and engage directly with your audience. Transparent and interactive social media presence can significantly boost your brand's trustworthiness among Generation Alpha.

Listening is equally important. Use surveys, forums, and social media analytics to understand what matters most to Generation Alpha. Analyse their concerns and aspirations, and let these insights guide your ethical marketing and CSR strategies. When they feel their voices are heard and acted upon, their loyalty towards your brand strengthens.

It's also beneficial to form alliances and partnerships that amplify your social responsibility impact. Collaborating with other businesses, NGOs, and governmental organisations can help you undertake larger initiatives that are more likely to have a substantial social impact. These collaborations can also make your efforts more credible and transparent.

Internally, fostering a culture that upholds these values is critical. Regular training and communication about your company's ethical marketing and CSR goals ensure that every employee from top to bottom is aligned and motivated to uphold these commitments. This creates an internal environment of integrity that naturally extends outward to your customer interactions.

As we move towards an increasingly global market, your ethical standards must reflect a sensitivity to diverse cultural contexts. What constitutes responsible marketing and social behaviour can vary across borders; hence, a one-size-fits-all approach may not be applicable. Tailor your strategies to resonate with the unique cultural and social landscapes of different regions while maintaining a unified corporate identity.

In conclusion, **Ethical Marketing and Social Responsibility** present a paradigm through which businesses can build lasting relationships with Generation Alpha. Their expectations are set high, but meeting them offers unmatched rewards in terms of loyalty, engagement, and brand value. By truly committing to transparency, inclusivity, and environmental and social responsibility, businesses can not only secure their place in the future market but also play a pivotal role in shaping a better world alongside Generation Alpha.

Chapter 14:
Shaping the Future Together

As we draw the curtains on this exploration, it's evident that the integration of Generation Alpha into our workplaces isn't just about accommodating another cohort. It's about recognising and harnessing the unique potential they bring to the table. By understanding their values, characteristics, and the unprecedented changes they will initiate, we position ourselves not just as passive participants, but as active architects of a transformative era.

One may ask, why all the fuss about Generation Alpha? The answer is simple: they're not just our future employees, but also our future leaders, innovators, and change-makers. Their immersion in technology, commitment to sustainability, and insistence on inclusivity means they will redefine how work gets done. Embracing their ethos gives us a preview of the future workplace - one that's seamless, dynamic, and interconnected.

Flexibility will be paramount. We've already seen the shift from conventional office spaces to hybrid models; what we've glimpsed is just the beginning. Generation Alpha will demand even more fluidity, where work is not a place you go, but an activity you engage in, irrespective of geography. This transition calls for not just structural changes, but a fundamental shift in mindset.

In this new world, innovation can't be a buzzword. It must be woven into the fabric of our organisational cultures. Leaders will be tasked with fostering environments where creativity thrives, where risk-taking is encouraged, and where failures are seen as learning opportunities rather than setbacks. The organisational champions of the future will be those who cultivate an atmosphere where Generation Alpha feels empowered to experiment and innovate.

Perhaps the most profound shift we'll see is in the realm of technology. Generation Alpha's familiarity with AI, blockchain, and virtual reality will render these technologies as indispensable as email or the internet is today. Our challenge will be to integrate these tools ethically and responsibly, ensuring that they enhance, rather than replace, human efforts. The leaders who succeed will be those who balance technological prowess with a human touch.

Let's talk about sustainability. For Generation Alpha, this isn't just a preference; it's a non-negotiable. They don't just want green offices; they expect businesses to be stewards of the environment. This commitment will extend beyond superficial nods to compliance and delve into authentic, measurable actions that address environmental and social responsibility. Companies willing to lead in this space will earn not only the loyalty of their younger employees but also the respect of an increasingly socially-conscious consumer base.

Leadership paradigms are evolving, and with Generation Alpha at the helm, adaptability and empathy will take precedence. Gone are the days of rigid hierarchies; in their place, we'll see networks of empowered teams, each contributing to a shared vision. Successful leaders will be those who can navigate these networks with emotional intelligence, understanding the nuanced needs of their teams, and guiding them to collective success.

The continuous learning ethos will underpin the success of Generation Alpha. This cohort values growth and development, and they'll seek out employers who prioritise lifelong learning. Employers must invest in their people, providing opportunities for both formal and informal education, and leveraging new platforms and technologies to facilitate learning. By doing so, they don't just retain talent; they cultivate it.

Furthermore, the gig economy will shape the employment landscape. Flexibility and autonomy appeal greatly to Generation Alpha, and organisations must adapt to cater to this preference. The traditional employer-employee relationship will evolve, with freelancing and gig roles becoming more prominent. This shift will necessitate new frameworks for support and protection, ensuring that both freelancers and employers benefit mutually from these dynamic arrangements.

Diversity, equity, and inclusion (DEI) will no longer be optional. Organisations that genuinely embrace DEI will stand out to Generation Alpha. Beyond tokenistic gestures, these efforts must be ingrained in the company ethos, influencing everything from hiring practices to daily interactions. By creating truly inclusive workplaces, we not only drive innovation but also foster an environment where everyone feels valued and empowered.

Health and well-being will be integral to workplace success. Mental and physical health considerations will be paramount, with leaders playing a crucial role in fostering environments that support both. Flexible schedules, ergonomic setups, and mental health resources will be essential in ensuring that employees can bring their best selves to work every day.

Legal and ethical considerations, particularly around data privacy and AI, will need vigilant oversight. The digital age brings unparalleled opportunities but also significant responsibilities. Ethical transparency and robust data protection mechanisms will be crucial in building trust, both within the organisation and with its external stakeholders. Leaders must balance efficiency with ethical imperatives, ensuring that progress doesn't come at the cost of principles.

Finally, the unpredictable nature of the future means that resilience and adaptability will be invaluable. Scenario planning and agile methodologies will be key in navigating the uncertainties ahead. Organisations that foster a culture of experimentation, learning from both their successes and failures, will be well-equipped to handle whatever the future holds.

The global workforce will present both challenges and opportunities. Managing cross-cultural teams and leveraging diverse talents will be crucial in maintaining a competitive edge. Effective communication and cultural understanding will be essential tools in bridging geographical distances and fostering trust within remote teams.

In conclusion, the future isn't a distant reality - it's a present opportunity. Embracing Generation Alpha means staying ahead of the curve, not just by understanding their characteristics, but by genuinely integrating their values and expectations into our organisational fabrics. By doing so, we shape a future that's innovative, inclusive, and sustainable. Let's embark on this journey together, with optimism and a shared commitment to shaping a better tomorrow.

Appendix A:
Resources for Further Learning

As we stand on the cusp of integrating Generation Alpha into the workplace, continuous education and access to resources become critical. This appendix is dedicated to providing you with a curated list of platforms, readings, and tools that will help you stay ahead in understanding and adapting to the emerging trends. These resources have been meticulously chosen to align with the core values, technological advancements, and cultural shifts discussed throughout this book.

Books and Publications

"The Fourth Industrial Revolution" by Klaus Schwab - A comprehensive examination of how technological advancements are reshaping industries, economies, and societies.

"Leaders Eat Last" by Simon Sinek - Insights into new leadership paradigms emphasising empathy, trust, and collaboration, which are essential for managing Generation Alpha.

"Educated" by Tara Westover - A memoir that highlights the significance of continuous learning and adaptability, providing a personal perspective on lifelong education.

"Sapiens: A Brief History of Humankind" by Yuval Noah Harari - An exploration of humanity's history that offers valuable context for understanding the future workplace dynamics.

"Cradle to Cradle: Remaking the Way We Make Things" by William McDonough and Michael Braungart - A key read for those looking to integrate sustainable practices into their organisational frameworks.

Online Courses and Platforms

Coursera - Offers a wide array of courses on leadership, technology, and innovation from top universities and companies. Courses such as "Leading for Equity, Diversity and Inclusion in Higher Education" and "AI For Everyone" are particularly beneficial.

edX - Another excellent platform providing courses in collaboration with universities like MIT and Harvard. Look for classes like "Tech for Good: The Role of ICT in Achieving the SDGs."

LinkedIn Learning - Perfect for time-crunched professionals, offering bite-sized learning modules on topics ranging from emotional intelligence to remote team management.

FutureLearn - Specialises in courses that focus on social responsibility and ethical leadership, crucial for shaping inclusive and sustainable workplaces.

Webinars and Online Communities

TED Talks - A treasure trove of short, impactful discussions. Search for talks on leadership, sustainability, and the future of work to get inspired and informed.

HR.com - Comprehensive webinars and virtual conferences that provide insights into modern HR practices. Topics often cover evolving workplace dynamics and the integration of emerging generations.

Reddit's r/Futurology - A vibrant community where forward-thinking leaders share articles, discuss trends, and debate the impact of technological advancements.

Industry Reports and Whitepapers

Deloitte Insights - Regularly publishes forward-looking reports on topics such as the future of work and inclusive leadership practices.

McKinsey Global Institute - Offers detailed whitepapers that provide data-driven insights into emerging technologies and workforce trends.

World Economic Forum - Access their extensive library of reports on the intersection of global economic trends and technological advancements.

PwC's Workforce of the Future - A must-read to help you understand how demographics, technology, and socio-economic factors shape the future workplace.

Professional Associations

Society for Human Resource Management (SHRM) - Provides resources, training, and certification opportunities for HR professionals aiming to stay current with industry standards.

Association for Talent Development (ATD) - Focuses on personal and professional development, offering resources that can help in everything from leadership development to incorporating new technologies.

Chartered Institute of Personnel and Development (CIPD) - A British-based organisation providing a wealth of resources on people management and development, particularly suited for those navigating multi-generational teams.

Each of these resources offers unique insights and practical tools that you can incorporate into your daily practices. Engaging with these materials will not only keep you informed but also inspired to create a workplace where Generation Alpha can thrive. Stay curious, keep learning, and remember that the future is being shaped by the actions and knowledge we cultivate today. Empower yourself and your organisation to step confidently into the era of Generation Alpha.

Glossary of Terms

Agile Methodologies: A set of principles and practices aimed at building adaptive and flexible project management and software development approaches. Emphasises iterative progress, collaboration, and the capacity to adapt to change.

AI (Artificial Intelligence): Technology that simulates human intelligence through machines, particularly computers. Utilised in various workplace functions, from automation to decision-making.

Augmented Reality (AR): A technology that overlays digital information, such as images, sounds, or other data, on the real world through devices like smartphones or AR glasses.

Blockchain: A decentralised digital ledger system used for recording transactions across numerous computers. Prominent for its transparency and security, particularly relevant for financial and supply chain management.

Corporate Social Responsibility (CSR): A company's commitment to managing its business processes in a way that produces a positive impact on society. Includes environmental, social, and economic responsibilities.

DEI (Diversity, Equity, and Inclusion): A framework aimed at promoting fair treatment and full participation of all individuals within an organisation. Focuses on creating workplaces that value diverse perspectives and ensure equitable opportunities for all.

Digital Natives: Generations that have grown up with digital technology such as the Internet, computers, and smartphones. Generation Alpha is often categorised as digital natives.

Emotional Intelligence (EI): The capability to recognise, understand, manage, and reason with emotions in oneself and others. Seen as essential for effective leadership and collaboration in the workplace.

Ethical Considerations: The evaluation of actions and decisions based on moral principles and values, particularly in areas like AI and data privacy.

Gig Economy: A labour market characterised by short-term contracts or freelance work, as opposed to permanent jobs. Offers flexibility but also presents challenges in job security and benefits.

Generation Alpha: The cohort born from approximately 2010 onwards, marked by their comfort with technology, strong values around sustainability, and high expectations for workplace adaptability.

Green Offices: Workspaces designed to be environmentally friendly, focusing on reducing energy consumption, waste, and promoting sustainability in office operations.

Hybrid Models: Work arrangements that combine elements of remote and in-office work, offering employees greater flexibility and promoting work-life balance.

Inclusive Workplaces: Environments that actively welcome and support diversity, ensuring that all employees have equal opportunities and feel valued.

Microlearning: An educational approach that delivers content in small, specific bursts, allowing for focused learning on particular topics or skills. Often supported by digital platforms.

Remote Work: A work arrangement where employees perform their job duties from locations outside the traditional office setting, often facilitated by digital communication tools.

Sustainability: The principle of meeting current needs without compromising the ability of future generations to meet theirs. Involves practices that promote environmental health, social well-being, and economic viability.

Virtual Reality (VR): A technology that enables users to experience and interact with a computer-generated environment in a seemingly real way, often via headsets.

Work-Life Balance: The equilibrium between personal life and professional work, aimed at ensuring that neither domain adversely affects the other. Efforts to achieve this balance often focus on flexible schedules and supportive work environments.

www.ingramcontent.com/pod-product-compliance
Lightning Source LLC
Chambersburg PA
CBHW030004190526
45157CB00014B/411